Screenplay Competitions

Tools and Insights to Help You Choose the Best Screenwriting Contests for You and Your Script

by Ann Marie Williams

published by
Bluestocking Press
www.bluestockingpress.com

Published by Bluestocking Press
Placerville, California
www.bluestockingpress.com

Printed and bound in the United States of America

Edited by Jane A. Williams and Tyler A. Schade

Library of Congress Cataloging-in-Publication Data

Names: Williams, Ann Marie, 1983- author.
Title: Screenplay competitions : tools and insights to help you choose the best screenwriting contests for you and your script / Ann Marie Williams.
Description: Placerville, California : Bluestocking Press, [2019] | Includes index.
Identifiers: LCCN 2018054901 | ISBN 9780942617757 (softcover)
Subjects: LCSH: Motion picture authorship--Competitions.
Classification: LCC PN1996 .W45 2019 | DDC 808.2/3079--dc23
LC record available at https://lccn.loc.gov/2018054901

ISBN: 978-0-942617-75-7

To my parents.
I love you both.

Contents

Why I Wrote This Book

In 2013, when I first began entering screenwriting competitions, I knew very little about the competition process. I knew that I wanted to find out how my script stacked up against the competition, and I knew that I wanted to retain all rights to my work.

But that was about all I knew.

I didn't understand the judging process or that it varied from competition to competition. I wasn't aware of the different eligibility requirements pertaining to myself as a writer and the script I wanted to enter. I had no idea that so many varying types of written critiques were available. And I certainly didn't know that being a quarterfinalist in one competition meant something entirely different from being a quarterfinalist in another.

However, over the course of a few years (and dollars spent) I learned.

And the more I came to understand how screenwriting competitions worked, the more I realized that I didn't have to win competitions to benefit from them.

That realization drastically changed how I approached the entire screenwriting competition process because I learned that I could turn that process into an educational one that would help improve not only my script and my writing, but also *myself as a writer*.

Screenwriting competitions offer experiences and situations that writers aren't exposed to by the actual act of writing. Going through the screenwriting competition process helped me learn how to deal with disappointment, success, and deadlines. It helped me learn how to be patient and how to set one project aside and move on to another. I've become comfortable reading legalize because every competition I enter requires me to do so. And the competition process helped me learn to analyze and deal with critiques.

And the best part: All those benefits are within my control.

Don't get me wrong, winning is great! And it can happen. But I know the odds of winning—or even placing highly—are incredibly small. Moreover, I've learned that different competitions reward script qualities differently.

Of the competitions listed in *Screenplay Competitions*, I've been a quarterfinalist in Scriptapalooza's International Screenplay Competition in the sci-fi genre. I've also been a quarterfinalist in the ScreenCraft Family-Friendly Screenplay Contest (top 25%) and a semifinalist (top 8%) in their inaugural Sci-Fi Screenplay Contest. I've been a semifinalist (top 2%) in the Austin Film Festival Screenplay Competition in the sci-fi genre, and a sci-fi finalist in the 2017 Nashville Film Festival Screenwriting Competition (top 4%). (If you're confused by the differing percentages, don't worry. So was I. I'll explain the terminology and percentages in greater detail in the "Advancement" portion of Section I.)

However, those same scripts failed to make it past the second round at PAGE and never got anywhere at Nicholl, Big Break®, BlueCat, or Script Pipeline.

So, unfortunately, I can't tell you which competitions you should enter, or even that you *should* enter competitions. Each competition is different—and so is each writer and each script.

But, I can explain the competition process (and how it varies among competitions) so that you can be better equipped to make those selections yourself, hopefully saving you time, money and a lot of confusion.

To help do this, I've selected a handful of competitions to include in *Screenplay Competitions* as way of reference and example. However, if I reference a competition in this book, it does not mean I think you should (or should not) enter that competition. Nor does it mean that these are the only competitions worth entering. Instead, the reasons I selected these competitions are three-fold:

1. They provide an overview of the similarities and differences among competitions.

2. Most of the competitions selected appear on several "top screenwriting competition" lists and are often perceived as some of the most reputable in the industry.

3. I have entered my own scripts into at least one of the competitions offered by each of the referenced competition organizations.

I should also mention that I've been fortunate enough to experience the screenwriting competition process from the judge's perspective. As a result of being a semifinalist in the Austin Film Festival Screenplay & Teleplay Competition (AFF), I was asked to be one of their Readers (someone who judges for initial rounds of their competition). Not only did this allow me to experience competitions from the perspective of a judge, it gave me new insights into how to evaluate my own writing.

So, through all this firsthand experience, I've learned that it's important to select competitions that are reputable and have earned the respect of the film industry. But, in addition to this, it's important to identify which of those competitions are most likely to reward the type of script I've written, as well as those competitions from which I can learn the most.

I still enter screenwriting competitions with the *hope* of winning, but my *goal* is to use the competition process to better my script, my writing, and myself as a writer. If I can do that, then the time and money I spend entering competitions becomes more than a chance at winning—it becomes an investment in myself. And that moves me closer to a screenwriting career—whether I win the competition or not.

It is my sincere hope that *Screenplay Competitions* will help you do the same.

Terminology

One of the reasons the screenwriting competition process can be so confusing is due to terminology. Even though most competitions use the same terminology, their *definitions* of the terms aren't consistent. What one competition calls a "judge" another competition calls a "reader." Where one competition's quarterfinalists represent the top 25% of entries, another competition's quarterfinalists represent the top 15%.

So, in an attempt to avoid confusion, I've included a glossary in *Screenplay Competitions* to clarify how terms are defined *for purposes of this book.* Throughout these pages, when a term that appears in the glossary is first introduced or defined in the text, the term is displayed in bold typeface.

Competitions Referenced

Below is a list of the competitions referenced in *Screenplay Competitions*. The official title of the competition appears first, followed by its acronym or abbreviated title, any of which may be used throughout the text of this book.

1. Academy Nicholl Fellowships in Screenwriting (Nicholl)
2. Austin Film Festival Screenplay & Teleplay Competition (AFF)
3. BlueCat Screenplay Competition (BlueCat)
4. Final Draft®'s Big Break® Screenwriting Contest (Big Break®)
5. Nashville Film Festival Screenwriting Competition
6. The Page International Screenwriting Awards (PAGE)
7. ScreenCraft *runs multiple format and genre-specific competitions per year.*
8. Scriptapalooza International Television Writing Competition & Scriptapalooza International Screenplay Competition
9. Script Pipeline Screenwriting Competition (Script Pipeline)
10. Sun Valley Film Festival High Scribe Screenplay Competition

Disclaimer

Although accurate at the time of this writing, competition rules, eligibility requirements, terms and conditions, privacy policies, awards, prizes, judging criteria, etc. can change with the click of a button, so always research each competition thoroughly prior to entering so you have the most current information and understand what you are agreeing to by entering.

Reasons to Enter Screenwriting Competitions

Entering a screenwriting competition with the hope of winning is a great goal. However, statistically, the chance of winning a screenwriting competition is *incredibly* small. Even if you've written a stellar script, the odds of making it through multiple rounds of competition (where multiple judges must agree on the merits of your script) is not very high. It can happen! But, if it doesn't, it is nice to realize that you can still benefit from the competition process.

As I mentioned earlier, my original reason for entering screenwriting competitions was to determine where my script and my writing stacked up compared to other scripts. But, over time, I began to realize that competitions and the competition process could offer additional benefits. What follows is a list of those benefits. And while not every competition will offer every benefit, knowing which benefits you're seeking will help you select the right competitions for you and your script.

Career Advancement

One reason to enter screenwriting competitions is to advance a screenwriting career. Writers may hope that if they enter a competition and win or **place** (do not win, but **advance** to certain levels in the competition), they will be called into meetings with agents, managers, and producers. They will sell their spec script for hundreds of thousands of dollars and end up a highly sought after screenwriter.

That's not an impossible goal. It can happen. But the odds are not in our favor. Some competitions receive over 7,000 **entries** each year but select only a handful of winners.

And, even if you win a competition, the win alone does not guarantee a screenwriting career.

One reason for this is that some competitions generate more "buzz" for their winning scripts than other competitions. Most competitions' websites include a "success stories" type section. Check those out. Research the competition winners (and those who placed). How much did winning (or placing) in that competition affect their careers? Were the winning scripts produced? Have you heard of the movie or television show? Did the writers sign with agents or managers? Are they working, paid screenwriters today? These are all clues regarding how successful a competition has been at selecting talented writers, finding marketable scripts, and/or helping their winners achieve a screenwriting career.

But, in addition to this, a writer's career success depends on more than just the film industry's interest generated by winning the competition. Even if you win a prestigious competition it is up to you to make the most of that win. Competitions can open doors, but you have to be willing and prepared to walk through them. A winning script might be extraordinarily good, but if the writer isn't willing to work with producers, or doesn't understand the business side of the industry, then that script might never make it off the page.

Nevertheless, winning screenwriting competitions *can* be a legitimate path to a screenwriting career. Just be aware that you will still have to take a lot of steps once that path stretches out before you.

Exposure

One way screenwriting competitions help advance writers' careers is by providing exposure for their winners (or finalists, etc.). Whether the competition circulates your script's **logline**, arranges for you to meet with industry insiders, or pitches your script to a list of agents and producers who might be interested in your script, winning (or placing in) a competition can have the potential to help you get a foot in the door.

Credentials

If you win or place in screenwriting competitions (or even if a critique of your script garners a "recommend"), you can opt to use these results in your query letters or pitches. Doing so informs the recipient that you've already been "vetted and approved" by someone in the industry.

However, before you decide to include these types of credentials in your queries/pitches, you will want to consider how much time has passed since you received them. If too much time has passed, mentioning a competition win or placement might be a detriment more than an asset.

You'll also want to consider if the credential pertains to you as a writer *or* a specific script. If you're trying to get hired as a writer, then mentioning a competition win could help validate your skill as a writer. However, if you're trying to sell "Script A," then mentioning a competition win for "Script B" could leave people wondering why "Script A" *hasn't* won a competition.

Finally, you'll want to consider the prestige of the competition and how highly you placed within it. Winning a less prestigious competition might not add much credibility to your pitch or query letter. But being a quarterfinalist at a highly respected competition might. Similarly, receiving a positive judge's comment may or may not be worth mentioning, depending on the credentials of that judge.

Mentorship

Mentorship is often about either helping the writer learn how to navigate the film industry, and/or helping to improve the writer's script and/or writing abilities as a whole.

Many screenwriting competitions do not award any type of mentorship, but for those that do, the types of mentorship vary significantly. Mentorships can come in a variety of forms, from fellowships (lasting anywhere from a week to a year), to exclusive classes offered as part of a competition's corresponding festival, to a single phone call that lasts an hour.

Mentorship can be very beneficial, but it's important to understand what type of mentorship the competition offers, how long it will last, who the mentor/s will be, and if you'll have the time and funds available to participate (since travel or relocation may be required, and sometimes at your expense).

Money

Many screenwriting competitions offer a monetary prize to winners, which can vary from a few hundred dollars to over thirty thousand dollars.

Money isn't always part of the prize. But, when it is, money is rarely the only prize offered. Moreover, some competitions offer other potentially money-saving prizes, such as free festival passes, free writing software, memberships to writing websites and online communities, magazine subscriptions, stipends for travel and lodging, etc.

I don't recommend entering competitions for the sole purpose of winning money, but it can be a nice addition to the other benefits and opportunities a win might bring.

Learning Your Script's Rank

Learning where your script **ranks** among thousands of other entries can be very helpful for new writers, as well as established writers who want to get reactions to a new script. You might discover that your script fares better than you expected. Or, it might fare worse. But, whatever the result, how far your script advances in a competition (or preferably *competitions*) can provide insight regarding the amount of work your script, or your writing skills, still need.

Critiques

Knowing how your script ranks is helpful. But knowing *why* it ranked the way it did can be even more beneficial.

Given the nature of the screenwriting competition process, every judge must critique (evaluate) a script in order to rank it, whether that critique is written down or mentally recorded. As such, every **entrant** of a competition will receive, at minimum, this critique: *either your script advances in the competition or it does not.*

However, many competitions do offer some form of ***written* critique** (a written explanation of the strengths and weaknesses of your script). The length of the critique, the cost, the content, the credentials of the individual who writes your critique, as well as when you will receive the critique all vary from competition to competition.

Depending on the competition, some critiques will be written by your script's competition judge (or judges), and some will be written by another individual. In either case, written critiques can offer valuable insight into the strengths and weaknesses of your *script* and your abilities as a *writer*. Even if you don't win a competition, the accompanying critiques can make entering the competition worthwhile.

As helpful as critiques can be to your writing and to your script, learning how to *deal* with critiques (good or bad) is a skill that's crucial for every writer. All the critiques in the world won't help you improve if you don't know how to digest, analyze, and benefit from them. So, since I value the educational aspect of competitions as much as I do the potential for exposure, I've devoted an entire section to critiques (Section III), covering the types of critiques available and ways to deal with them.

Deadlines

Do you need deadlines to help you write? Don't know? By entering a competition, you can determine if having an entry deadline helps or hurts your writing.

Moreover, if you want a screenwriting career, odds are excellent that you'll have to write to deadlines eventually. You may as well start getting used to them now.

Motivation

Entering screenwriting competitions, getting results and critiques, and knowing that there's the *possibility* you could win can be fun and exciting—a welcome feeling after the weeks, months, and sometimes years of perfecting your script.

Writing can be a long, solitary process and even professional writers occasionally feel stuck and question why they write. So, if the goal of entering a competition gives you the extra motivation to push through those painful rewrites, or if the idea of someone else reading your script fans the flame of excitement and makes final edits just a little easier, then competitions might provide the incentive you need to see you through the tougher aspects of writing.

Validation

If you do well in a screenwriting competition, or if you make it past the first **round** of judging, or even if you just get a few good comments in a critique, a positive reaction to your script can validate that you're not entirely crazy for trying to make a go of a screenwriting career.

The degree of validation you receive, and the number of sources that provide it, will help you better understand where your writing currently stands, and how much work you may still need to do on your script.

Maybe you realize it's more work than you want to do—and that's fine. Perhaps you're not passionate enough about that specific story to see you through multiple rewrites.

Or maybe you realize that you're actually eager to start rewriting because you believe in yourself, you believe in your script, and you're willing to put in the work to make your script the best version it can be.

Whatever the outcome, information is a good thing. I strongly suggest, however, that if you're going to enter competitions (or request critiques) you enter your script in *at least two competitions* (or receive *at least two critiques*). Entering multiple competitions and receiving multiple critiques is really a kindness to yourself because there is a subjective aspect to judging and critiquing scripts. The more insights you receive from multiple sources, the more accurately you'll be able to assess where your script and your writing stand—where they excel, and where they need improvement (because, as I see it, there is always room for improvement).

Summary

Going through the screenwriting competition process offers a variety of situations that you can use to help you become a better *writer*—not just improving your ability to write, but improving your approach to writing and certain aspects of a writing career.

Competitions provide the opportunity for you to learn how to deal with deadlines, disappointment, and success. Competitions require patience. Competitions provide an introduction to legal lingo. And competitions provide you with the opportunity to learn how to *deal with* critiques.

Many factors affect a script's advancement in a competition and many of these factors are not in the writer's control. However, there are goals you can control, goals that are your responsibility to achieve and that *are* achievable.

My goal for *Screenplay Competitions* is to help you identify your goals and identify the competitions most likely to help you achieve them.

The Five Steps of Screenplay Competitions

The screenplay competition process typically includes five basic steps: accept, read, rank, advance, award. Each step will be covered in greater detail throughout this book, but I want to begin with a brief description of each step.

Accept

Competitions accept entries (sometimes referred to as *submissions*) to be judged.

Entries to screenplay competitions are usually in the form of *full and complete scripts*. However, other types of competitions accept concepts, treatments, loglines, or partial scripts (e.g. the first thirty pages of a script).

Read

Once submitted to the competition, every script is read, either in full or in part, by at least one competition **judge** (sometimes referred to as a *reader*).

The qualifications and credentials of judges can vary from competition to competition and from round to round.

Rank

Once a script is read, it is ranked by its judge (or judges).

The rank/s assigned to the script is/are used to determine if the script advances in the competition or not.

The number of judges required to rank a script before that script can be advanced (or eliminated) varies from competition to competition (and sometimes round to round within a competition).

Competitions often provide judges with **judging criteria**—specific categories (like character, plot, structure, pacing, etc.) to evaluate a script's strengths and weaknesses.

Once a judge determines the strengths and weaknesses of a script, that judge must convert those determinations into a quantifiable ranking. The type of **quantifiers** used varies from competition to competition—and sometimes from round to round *within* a competition. However, rankings are typically quantified either by scores, recommendations, comments, and/or discussions.

Advance

Scripts that receive an advancing rank move on to the next round of competition.

These scripts are read and ranked again. Each script is typically assigned to a judge (or judges) who did not read the script in a previous round.

These new rankings (either alone, or in combination with the rankings from the previous round/s) are used to determine which scripts advance to the next round.

This process is repeated for however many rounds a competition requires until the final round of the competition is reached. At that point, the remaining scripts are read and ranked again. Those rankings (either alone or in conjunction with these scripts' rankings from previous rounds) determine the competition's winner (or winners).

While many competitions use multiple rounds of competition before selecting winners, some competitions might only have *one* round of judging in which all entries are read and ranked, and from that pool the winner/s is/are chosen. This doesn't mean one method is better or fairer, but if you're trying to determine where your script stacks up against the competition, knowing how many rounds your script advanced through can offer more insight than only finding out if your script did or did not win.

Award

Some competitions award one winner. Others award multiple winners. A few competitions award one first place winner, but also award second and third place winners. And several competitions award a winner for each **format**, **genre**, or **category** they judge.

Winning a competition (and sometimes placing highly) is often accompanied by prizes. Competition prizes vary significantly but might consist of: cash, software, gift cards, subscriptions, memberships, script or logline circulation, consultations, mentorships, festival or conference tickets/passes, promotion of you or your script, and so forth.

Before you enter any competition, be sure you understand and are willing to accept the awards and prizes offered. Awards and prizes sometimes include option deals, guaranteed representation, or other prizes that will affect the rights, ownership, and/or production of your script as well as your ability to enter other competitions or fellowships.

It's equally important to know if *entering* a competition in any way affects your intellectual rights. So, though I will later discuss eligibility requirements and **fine print**, I want to emphasize now that you should read and understand all the terms, conditions, rules, guidelines, agreements, etc., that a competition requires you to agree and adhere to if you enter.

Section I

The Competition Process

Most screenwriting competitions operate in a similar fashion. Entries are read and judged, a select few scripts are advanced to the next round, those scripts are read and judged again, still fewer advance, and so forth, until winning scripts are selected.

But how does that process actually happen? How are scripts judged? What **criteria** do the judges use to rank scripts? Who are the judges? What are the judges' credentials? How many judges read and rank your script? And how many rounds must your script advance through in order to be considered for the win?

This section will take you through the actual competition process so that you have a better idea of how competitions work and what to expect after you've finalized your **submission**.

Note: I'll discuss in detail the **submission process** (also called the entry process or application process) in Section VI, but first I want to explain what happens to your entry after it's submitted *so that you can make a more informed decision regarding which competitions you want to enter.*

1

After You Click Submit

Let's assume you decide to enter your script in a competition. You've completed the submission process. Now what? What happens to your script after you click "submit"?

Numbering Scripts

Most likely your script will be assigned a unique number that is used to identify your script during the judging process.

It's not uncommon for more than one script to have the same title, so assigning numbers to scripts helps eliminate any "title confusion" that may arise. This becomes especially important for those competitions that remove (or require entrants to remove) writers' names and contact information from scripts. The removal of names and contact information is often required because the competitions do not want judges to know entrants' names or locations in order to avoid any potential author-related bias (e.g. name recognition, gender, age, ethnicity, etc.).

This doesn't mean competitions that allow you to leave identifying information on your script *are* biased. But if entrants' names and contact information are removed, the question becomes irrelevant.

Judge Assignment

Once a script is numbered, it's assigned to a judge or judges. But how do competitions determine which judges get which scripts? And how do the judges actually access those scripts?

Judge Preferences

Some competitions assign scripts to judges who have an affinity for those scripts' genres and **tones**. Personally, I like when this happens because:

1. Your judge already enjoys the genre of your script. Even though judges should be able to set their personal preferences aside, it seems more probable that your romantic comedy script will fare better if read by a judge who enjoys the romantic comedy genre. Or said differently, you're less likely to have a judge love your romantic comedy if he/she despises the romantic comedy genre.

2. A judge who enjoys a genre will likely be more familiar with other scripts and films/shows in that genre and should, therefore, be better equipped to bring critical analysis to your script relative to that genre. This can be especially helpful if you're getting a written critique from that judge.

3. Having been a judge, I was grateful that I could request scripts in genres that I enjoyed. Moreover, I was better qualified to read and rank scripts in genres and tones with which I was familiar.

Number of Scripts Assigned

The number of scripts each judge is required to read during the competition varies from competition to competition, and sometimes round to round.

One could argue that the fewer scripts a judge reads, the fresher and more excited the judge will be, resulting in fairer and more thorough rankings and critiques. But one could also argue that the judge who reads hundreds of scripts per **competition year** is better equipped to judge, rank, and critique each script relative to all the others.

Ideally, judges should be skilled enough and professional enough that the *quantity* of scripts they read for a competition makes no difference in their ability to evaluate scripts.

Script Access

Once scripts are assigned, judges can begin reading those scripts. But how do the judges actually *receive* your script?

Scripts might be printed (or received in paper format) and read by judges at the competition's office or "checked out" by judges locally.

Or, judges might access electronically submitted scripts online, after which the scripts are either read online, downloaded to computer desktops (or tablets, smartphones, etc.), or printed to paper.

I fully realize how scary this sounds. When you enter a competition, you are putting your script out there (often into cyberspace). And even if the competition states you will retain the rights to your script, risk is a part of the cyber world.

So, to help protect my work, I copyright all my scripts with the United States Government Copyright Office prior to submitting them to any competition or **critique service**.

While typically not required, most competitions do encourage writers to copyright their work and/or register their work with the Writer's Guild of America.

2

The Judges

So, who are the judges exactly? And what makes them qualified to evaluate your script?

Terminology

It's common for competitions to use the term judge *and/or* the term **reader** to refer to an individual who reads, evaluates, and ranks scripts in their competitions.

Why the two terms? It's not entirely clear.

Quite simply, it could be because "reader" doesn't sound quite as harsh as "judge."

Or, for those competitions that use both terms, it could be that the terms refer to different levels of judges and/or competition.

For example, perhaps a competition's initial rounds of judging are evaluated by script analysts and aspiring screenwriters, so the competition refers to these individuals as "readers." But perhaps the final round is evaluated by top film producers, so the competition refers to these individuals as "judges." This allows the competition to promote the high-profile status of their "judges," while still differentiating between them and the early round "readers."

Whatever the actual reason for the two terms, to avoid confusion within this book, I will use the term *judge* to refer to any individual who reads and ranks scripts during *any round of competition*. In other words, a judge is anyone whose evaluation of your script is used to determine (alone or in conjunction with other judges' rankings) your script's advancement in a competition.

Credentials

Judges have vastly different backgrounds and varying degrees of success and/or involvement in the film industry.

Judges might be managers, agents, or producers (from big studios or smaller ones). Judges might be script readers for production companies (again, big or small). Sometimes judges are individuals who are just starting out in the industry, and sometimes they are retired after a long career. Judges can also be administrators affiliated with the competition itself. Or, judges can be fellow writers (from aspiring to produced and award-winning). Some judges have years of experience judging competitions. Some have none.

Not only do judges credentials vary from competition to competition (and typically increase with each round of competition), sometimes the credentials of judges vary *within* a round of competition. For example, in the first round of competition one script might be judged by someone with ten years of judging experience, and another script might be judged by someone who has never judged a competition before. And, in most cases, you won't know who judged your script.

Even if a competition lists the names of their judges, it's unlikely you will know *which* of those judges read your script. With the exception of competitions promoting their high-profile judges (discussed shortly), typically judging is kept anonymous.

However, it is fairly common for a competition to post the *type* of credentials their judges must have in order to judge the competition. Some competitions take this a step further and list the required credentials relative to each *round* of the competition. And some competitions even provide the credentials of your script's judge *if* you receive a written critique from that judge (though it's still unlikely you will receive any personally identifying information about that judge).

All this begs the question: Do the judge's credentials matter?

Provided the judge is capable of evaluating a script's strengths and weaknesses relative to the competition's judging criteria, then it shouldn't matter relative to the competition's ability to select the winning/placing scripts.

However, some competitions indicate that their judges are currently working in the industry and are *actively seeking new writers or material*. This can be quite exciting because if these judges are evaluating initial rounds of competition then, by simply entering the competition, your script has the potential to be noticed by someone in the industry who might want to pursue the possibility of working with you.

But, separate from this, knowing your judges' credentials (or type of credentials) can help you determine if there's any consistency as to who advances your script and who does not. Do script readers generally rank your script well, but producers do not? Do fellow screenwriters score your script highly, but agents don't? Moreover, if a working film producer advances or eliminates your script then you might choose to put more weight on that decision than one that came from a fellow aspiring screenwriter.

And this brings me back to the point I touched on before: Sometimes competitions actively promote the identity or credentials of high-profile judges. While this sounds exciting, it's unlikely that those high-profile judges are reading *every script* entered in the competition. Instead, it is more likely that these high-profile judges only evaluate scripts that reach the final round/s of competition. Therefore, your script will typically need to advance through several rounds of competition before that high-profile judge would ever have the opportunity to read your script.

Compensation

Some judges get paid, some do not. Some are compensated monetarily and some receive non-cash compensation (e.g. free conference passes, festival tickets). Some competitions might compensate initial round judges but not those who judge the final rounds. Others might do the opposite.

Some judges are actively seeking new scripts to produce or writers to represent or manage, so they judge competitions in order to find new material or writers. And some people judge in order to increase their screenwriting skills or to add experience to their resume.

Whatever the compensation, it's helpful to remember that not all judges get monetarily compensated for their time. So while it might be tempting to take umbrage with your judges (and sometimes they might deserve it), at the end of the day most judges are just trying to do their best to evaluate and critique scripts.

3

The Reading Process

Before a judge can evaluate a script, he/she must actually *read* the script. This is, of course, fairly obvious, but I'd like to make a few points regarding the reading process.

The Cold Read

When it comes time to read your script, usually the only information a judge will have about your script is the title. They are approaching your script "cold," as they say. Even if you've submitted a logline or summary to the competition along with your script, the judge will not necessarily see that logline or summary. Therefore, when you're editing your script, it's important to determine if you have enough story information in the first few pages to let your judge know where and when the story takes place. A judge might first be assigned a romantic comedy set in New York City in 2020, then a drama set in Boston in 1776, then a sci-fi set in an alternative universe. Imagine how confusing it can be to jump into each of those scripts not knowing when or where their stories take place.

This doesn't mean you can't have some mystery surrounding the location and era of your story, but the information you provide in the first few pages of your script should be clear enough that (at the very least) the judge can get a sense of how the story will look and sound once it's on the screen.

You can still build suspense and intrigue from the start. But if the judge doesn't understand what's supposed to be happening, then it's possible the script is creating *confusion* rather than building suspense and intrigue.

So read the first few pages of your script as objectively as you can, pretend you don't know what the story is about or where it's going, then determine if there is enough information on the page to let the reader know what he/she needs to know. If not, is there a reason (necessary to the story) why it isn't clear?

Amount of Script Read

Not every competition requires judges to read every script *in its entirety*.

It is likely that a judge *will* be required to read a script in its entirety in order to *advance* the script. However, some competitions allow judges to *eliminate* scripts after a predetermined minimum number of pages read (e.g. the first thirty pages).

I have mixed feelings about this.

Some scripts are so obviously unprepared for competition that a judge can tell in the first few pages that the script shouldn't advance. No matter how brilliant a plot is, or how well-drawn the characters are, if a script isn't formatted or structured properly, then there's no way it can (or should) advance. For these types of entries, it really isn't necessary for the judge to read the entire script.

However, as a writer, I prefer to know that my script will be read and judged in its entirety, so I typically gravitate to competitions that require a full read. Additionally, I've paid my entry fee just like everyone else, and for that reason my script should be given the same attention and consideration as all the others.

However, it takes time to read and judge scripts. The more pages a judge has to read, the more it costs the competition (if they are paying their judges), which could ultimately affect entry fees.

So, I understand both sides.

To win a competition, a script should be nearly perfect from start to finish. If a script has a stellar ending, but the beginning is sluggish, then odds are that script would not be worthy of winning the competition. Whether the judge was required to read the entire script or only the beginning, the script wouldn't win either way.

But, when it comes to advancing and placing in a competition, whether a script is read in it's entirety *can* matter, depending on how the competition advances scripts, and how many scripts they advance.

Let's say a screenwriter has two scripts: one has a great ending but a weak start, and one has a great start but a weak ending. Both are entered into a competition that allows judges to eliminate scripts at any point after the first thirty pages.

If the first round of eliminations is very steep (e.g. only 10% of scripts advance), then it's unlikely either script would advance. Whether the one script was eliminated after its weak start or the other script was eliminated after its weak ending, neither script would make the top 10%.

However, if the competition offers a more generous first cut (say, top 25%), then the script with a weak beginning but a great ending might not advance because the judge stopped reading after the weak beginning and, therefore, never read the ending that would have elevated the script as a whole. On the other hand, the script with a great beginning but a weaker ending might advance because the judge saw the merits of the beginning of the script even if the ending needed work.

Again, it's unlikely either script would win, but unless the scripts are assessed in their entirety, the initial cuts might not perfectly represent the "top 25%" of scripts. So, if you're trying to determine exactly how your script stacks up against the other entries, you might not get an accurate assessment unless all scripts are read in their entirety.

If you're getting a written critique from your script's judge/s, and your script is not read in its entirety, then the critique might not be as helpful as a critique based on your entire script (since the judge won't know how the story comes together at the end).

Additionally, I would argue that if you've paid *extra* for a critique, then the judge should be required to read the script in full. However, no script should be judged differently just because its entrant paid for a critique. So, when you're paying for a critique *from your judge*, the competition *should* already require all scripts to be read in their entirety. If this isn't clear, you might choose to contact the competition for clarification.

Number of Judges

The *number of script pages* a judge reads is only part of the equation. The *number of judges* required to read a script (or part of a script) in order for the script to be advanced or eliminated from the competition is the other part. For example:

- Competition A might require *one* judge's rank to determine if a script advances or is eliminated.

- Competition B might require *two* judges to rank a script and then total those two scores to determine advancement (or use only the better of the two scores to determine advancement).

- Competition C might require only one judge's rank to advance a script, but *two* judges' ranks to eliminate a script. So, if the first judge gives the script an advancing rank, the script advances. But if the first judge ranks the script for elimination, then the second judge has the opportunity to overturn or agree with that decision.

In some cases, *the number of script pages* a competition requires their judges to read might be dependant on *the number of judges* that are required to read the script. For example:

- Competition X might require only *one* judge to rank a script to determine advancement/elimination, but requires that the script be read *in its entirety* before that determination can be made.
- Competition Y might require the rank from only one judge to advance a script, but require the ranks from *two* judges to eliminate a script. However, while each judge might be required to read the entire script to advance it, they might each only be required to read the first thirty pages of the script to eliminate it.
- Competition Z might require one judge to read a script *in full* whether they rank it for advancement *or* elimination. But if that judge decides the script should be eliminated then a *second* judge must read the script and can either agree with the first judge or overturn the first judge's decision (thus advancing the script). While the second judge might be required to read the script *in its entirety* to overturn the first judge's decision, he/she might be required to read *only* the first thirty pages of the script in order to *agree* with the first judge (thus eliminating the script from the competition).

So, is one method better than the other? Personally, I like it when scripts are read in full and by at least two judges. But I understand why that isn't always necessary.

Whichever route a competition takes, it's always my preference that the competition clearly state its reading and judging process so that I understand what my entry fee is buying.

Timeline

Competitions generally begin the first round of judging shortly after they receive their earliest entries. This expedites the reading and judging process so that advancements (and their corresponding announcements) can be made in a timely manner after the competition closes for entries.

For example, a competition might open for entries on January 1st, close for entries on May 1st, and announce results on July 1st. If the competition receives thousands of entries, it could be impossible to judge them all in just two months. So, instead of waiting to begin judging until *after* May 1st, judging begins as soon as the first entries are received.

Depending on how a competition advances scripts, the second round of judging may or may not occur while the first round is still being completed. (How competitions advance scripts will be discussed in detail in Chapters 5 and 6.)

So, is there an advantage to enter your script in a competition earlier rather than later in the **submission period**?

One could argue that entering early gives your script an edge because the judges are fresh, excited, and aren't rushed or weighed down under the massive amount of scripts entered near the final deadline. Entering early could mean that the judges have the time to really read your script carefully (and give you thoughtful, comprehensive critiques—if they are required to provide critiques). There's also less chance the judge is comparing your script to that amazing script he/she read two months ago.

On the other hand, one could argue that entering early is a *disadvantage* because even though a judge might like your script, it's early in the competition and maybe he/she is "holding out," hoping to find a better script later on in the competition.

Of course, one could argue that the judges should be skilled enough to spot a stellar script regardless of the time-line. And most competitions state that the only difference between entering early and entering later is that it costs less to enter early (entry fees are discussed in Section VI).

Bottom line, you will receive no competitive advantage (assuming there is one) to enter your script early if you enter an unfinished or unpolished script. Personally, I want to enter the best version of my script so that I have the best chance to advance.

4

The Judging Process

Once a judge reads a script, he/she must evaluate and rank that script. Typically, there are two parts to this process:

1. The *judging criteria* the judge uses to evaluate scripts (discussed in this chapter).
2. The *quantifier/s* a judge uses to rank those evaluations (discussed in Chapter 5).

Format, Genre, and Category-Specific Judging

Before delving into the specifics of the judging process, I want to point out that many competitions use **format-specific judging**, **genre-specific judging**, and/or **category-specific judging**. This means scripts are judged *only* against other scripts *in the same format, genre or category* (instead of judging all entries against each other, regardless of format, genre or category).

Some competitions do this for all rounds of competition, others do this for specific rounds only. For example, all scripts might be judged together *regardless* of format, genre or category for the first two rounds of competition, but judged *per* format, genre or category for the final rounds of competition.

So how do you know what you're paying for when you enter a competition?

It's not always clear. I surmise that in *some* cases it might depend on whether each format, genre or category you enter your script under requires a *separate* entry fee. For example:

1. You decide to enter your script in Competition A's drama and sci-fi genres. Competition A requires you to pay a separate entry fee for *each* genre. In this example your script will likely be judged uniquely for the entire competition (receiving different judges for each genre).

2. You decide to enter your script in Competition B's drama and sci-fi genres. Competition B requires that you pay a full entry fee for one genre but a *discounted* fee for the second genre. In this example your script might *not* receive unique judges per genre (either for the entire competition or for certain rounds of the competition).

While either judging process can work, I find it helpful to know which process the competition I've entered implements so that I have a better idea of how many judges will read and rank my script.

Judging Criteria

Competitions often provide their judges with judging criteria (or guidelines). Judging criteria identifies the aspects of a script (as set forth by the competition) that should be used to evaluate each script's strengths and weaknesses.

Judging criteria helps ensure that all judges within a competition are evaluating and ranking scripts against the same standard (however, it is worth noting that a competition's criteria may vary per format, genre or category judged).

Judging criteria can vary from *competition to competition* in two ways:

1. The *criteria* that should be evaluated.

2. The *ranking emphasis* applied to each criterion.

First, while most competitions use much of the same criteria to evaluate scripts (plot, structure, character, etc.), some competitions include a few more unique judging criteria.

For example, Competition A might want to reward marketable scripts with big-budget concepts and wide-audience appeal. One of their judging criteria could be "marketability." Competition B, however, might want to reward scripts with a unique voice, a highly original plot, or an innovative concept. Consequently, Competition B might use "originality" as one of their judging criteria instead of "marketability."

Now, this isn't to say a script can't be *both* original *and* marketable, but it's important to know what you've written so you can enter competitions that are most likely to favorably rank (and thus hopefully advance) your script.

Secondly, while two competitions might use the same judging criteria, they might *weigh* each criterion differently.

For example, two different competitions might include plot, structure, and originality as part of their judging criteria. However, Competition A might require their judges to score plot, structure, and originality *individually* (thus putting equal emphasis on each criterion), while Competition B might *combine* plot and originality as one criterion, and structure as a separate criterion. Given this, if your script has a really great and original plot, but its structure is weak, then that script could end up with a different rank in these two competitions.

Several competitions provide their judging criteria, or a summary of it, online. I appreciate when competitions make this information available because I can evaluate my script against the competition's judging criteria and determine how I think my script would rank. Not only does this help me determine if I think the competition would be a good fit for my script, it also helps me identify the areas of my script that excel and the areas that need improvement.

However, not every competition will make their judging criteria public. And some competitions might not even provide their judges with judging criteria at all.

Furthermore, even if a competition publicly lists their judging criteria, it's rare for a competition to explain exactly what their judges are supposed to evaluate relative to that criteria. For example, a competition might list "story" as one of their judging criteria—but what does that mean exactly? Are they looking for an original plot? A unique twist on a classic tale? An emotionally engaging story? A marketable story?

Odds are the answer to each of the above questions is "yes"—but still, the less information available, the harder it is to determine which competitions are likely to look favorably upon your script, and thus the harder it is to determine in which competitions you should invest your time and money.

What follows is a list of the more common judging criteria I've encountered over the years, along with explanations of these criteria. But please note: *These are my explanations of the criteria.* Each competition will have slightly different definitions of these terms, and each competition will place different emphasis on the aspects of their criteria. However, my hope is that the following list and explanations give you an idea of the *types* of judging criteria used.

Even if these criteria and explanations don't exactly match the judging criteria of the competition/s you decide to enter, perhaps you'll discover criteria that you haven't yet used to evaluate your script, which might help you improve your script overall—and that's a good thing whether the competition uses that specific criterion or not.

As you read through the following criteria and explanations, you'll notice some overlap. This is because each aspect of a script affects every other aspect. Formatting is connected to pacing, pacing is connected to the plot, the plot is connected to the characters, and so on.

Concept/Premise

The concept or premise is the one idea that the story is built around. It is usually the focus of the logline. Typically, the concept is what sets the story in motion (the inciting incident/catalyst).

Competitions usually award high ranks to original concepts or those that have a fresh take or a unique twist on an existing motif.

Plot/Story

The plot is about the story itself; the events that unfold throughout the script.

When evaluating scripts against this criterion, judges might ask the following questions: Is the story plausible within the framework of the world created? Is the world engaging and absorbing? Is the story solid? Are there plot holes? Does every thread have a purpose? Do the subplots intertwine with the main plots? If you remove one subplot, does the story still hold? Is the story interesting? Exciting? Surprising? Unique? Is the plot a "page turner?" Is it emotionally engaging? Is it predictable? Do the twists and turns happen naturally and within the rules of the world, or do things happen conveniently? Does the setup for the story play out and pay off? Do the characters' actions drive the plot forward? If the story is a teleplay spec for an existing series, does the story fit the existing world while still conveying a unique storyline? If the script is a pilot for a new series, does the story demonstrate potential for multiple episodes/seasons?

Another aspect to consider when evaluating plot is how well the plot embodies the *concept*. For example, the concept for one of my scripts centered around a new world, the reason for its existence, and why people were sent there from their home world. However, in early drafts of that script, though the inciting incident served the concept (the protagonist was sent to the new world), the actual *plot* focused on uncovering a traitor (whose treason was related to a *secondary* concept in the script, not the main one). So, while interesting, the original traitor plot didn't leave me much room to explore the new world, the reason for its existence, and *thus the main premise*. Therefore, even though the original plot worked on its own, I had to set it aside because it didn't serve the main concept.

Structure

When I first began writing, it took me a while to identify the difference between plot and structure because the two terms are sometimes used interchangeably. However, for purposes of *Screenplay Competitions*: *plot* deals with the *story* while *structure* deals with the framework used to *convey* that story. So, the plot should convey your story's concept and the structure should convey your story's plot.

I think of it this way: Plot pertains to *what* the moments in your story *are*, structure pertains to *when* those moments *happen*. For example, *what* the inciting incident is falls under *plot*. *When* that inciting incident occurs in the story falls under *structure*.

To help determine the quality of a story's structure, judges might ask: Does the story make effective use of the structure implemented (e.g. three-act structure, linear, non-linear)? Is each act strong? Does the writer use descriptions, dialogue, transitions, etc., to build tension, pull the reader into the story, and propel them through the story at a good pace? Is it difficult to follow the story and/or is the story unnecessarily confusing? Is the story told in a logical, structurally appropriate way? (You can tell a story backwards if you want, provided it leads the reader in the right story direction.)

Another question to ask is: Does the climax actually resolve (or address) the main plot thread? If the answer is no, then you have to figure out if the plot has a problem (e.g. your main plot thread is never resolved) or the structure has a problem (e.g. what *should* be the climactic moment is in the wrong place in your script).

This is one reason why it's important to keep in mind that judges have to evaluate *the story that's on the page*. If you have a fantastic plot, but the structure doesn't convey that plot accurately or effectively, then the judges won't be able to discern how good the plot actually is.

For example, perhaps you've envisioned scene 81 as the climax—but you've positioned that scene too early. Because of this, scene 81 doesn't *read* like the climax, scene 93 does (maybe scene 93 is the climax of a subplot, which—while climactic—probably isn't nearly as exciting as scene 81 would have been). But the judge doesn't know this. The judge has to evaluate the story on the page, and that story is structured so that scene 93 is the climax.

Even though both plot points are addressed, the structure of the script doesn't do either of them justice, which could cause the judge to finish the script feeling underwhelmed.

Or perhaps the *climax* for the main plot comes at just the right time, but the *inciting incident* comes too late into the story, causing the reader to be unsure where the story is headed and what the resolution might be.

Formatting/Presentation

The difference between structure and formatting can seem nebulous at first. But I look at it this way: structure deals with the framework of your script; formatting deals with the tools you use to build that framework.

I don't mean paper versus parchment or Final Draft® versus Movie Magic®. I mean, did you use the proper formatting techniques (your tools) to tell your story?

Since a script is a written representation of a visual and auditory medium, the story on the *page* should be conveyed to the reader the same way the story on the *screen* will be conveyed to the audience—the same focus, the same pacing, the same impact. Screenwriting formatting tools are an effective way to help achieve that—to help you *effectively*, *efficiently*, and *accurately* convey your story as it will unfold on the screen.

For example, a scene heading typically has three or four pieces of information to convey the time and setting of a scene: interior or exterior, day or night, and location (which can range from very broad to very specific—e.g. New York City or Meredith's Kitchen).

While these brief pieces of information may seem constricting at first, they actually make for an effective method of conveying to the reader what the screen audience will experience.

The information in that one scene heading on the page (`INT. MEREDITH'S HOUSE - KITCHEN - DAY`) will be the first information coming at your screen audience at the start of that scene. And, if you think about it, that's how we typically process information. We see "the big picture" then the details. We see "it's a kitchen, it's daytime." Our minds process that before we see that Meredith is kneading the bread with a bit too much vigor or that the water was left running (the information that would come next in the narrative description).

And, yes, you could start a scene focused on the faucet, or the dough, and pan out to the kitchen. But, for the most part, we see the big picture first. Our minds process location and time of day without even realizing it, and that's how scene headings should work.

While scene headings might seem clunky and obtrusive at first, if the story is crafted well and the scene headings are used correctly, those scene headings become almost unnoticeable to the reader. The first time the story takes place in a location, we have to read (or look) a little more carefully to understand where we are. But when we know what's coming (when transitions are used effectively) or when the story's returning to a location already visited, we can almost gloss over the scene heading, the eyes flow easily and naturally with the progression of the story—just as the screen audience identifies a familiar or properly set-up setting without really knowing they are doing so. And all this allows the reader (or viewer) to focus on the action of the story and to stay emotionally invested in the story. In other words, scene headings are only obtrusive if they aren't used correctly. Used correctly, they aid in the conveyance and flow of the story.

In addition to scene headings, proper formatting helps keep the reader engaged in the story and in sync with the pacing in many other ways.

Imagine if a script (for no reason relative to the story itself) inconsistently refers to the protagonist Bob Smith as `BOB`, or `SMITH`, or `BOBBY SMITH`. This might not seem like a big deal—but it is. The inconsistency forces the reader to stop on the page and figure out which character you're referencing—and *the reader shouldn't have to figure it out.* That's the writer's job. And every time a reader has to stop reading your script to figure out your formatting problems, that reader is momentarily taken out of the story—the flow, the pacing, the world, and the emotion. And the more it happens, the harder it is to connect to the story and accurately evaluate its pace and structure.

Proper formatting requires that a certain amount of white space (a mix of description and dialogue) should appear on nearly every page of a script. Not only does this standard measure the number of minutes the story will be once filmed, but it is also an accurate way to convey the *pacing of the screen story on the page*. I will discuss pacing in detail soon, but I want to mention it here because formatting affects pacing: if one *second* of screen time takes one *minute* to read, then the story's pacing isn't accurately represented on the page.

This is one of the reasons why narrative description should be short and succinct, typically under four lines each. It keeps the script's focus on the main action or image, *which is all the viewing audience will have time to focus on*. Audiences won't have the time to focus on every decoration in Meredith's kitchen, and neither should the reader. Therefore, a description shouldn't be in a script unless it's important to the story.

When judging the formatting criterion, some screenwriting competitions focus solely on whether a script's formatting meets the standard screenplay or teleplay formatting requirements (e.g. spec vs. shooting format, correct font, type size, proper margins, proper use of scene headings, indentations, etc), as well as proper spelling and grammar (with the exception of a character that uses incorrect grammar when he/she speaks). But other competitions go beyond this, looking at the *craft* and *execution* of the story—evaluating whether the writer knows how to use the script format to convey a story effectively and efficiently. This can range from judging a writer's appropriate and effective use of transitions to judging a writer's ability to use the visual and auditory aspects of film to convey a story (the "show don't tell" idea).

As mentioned earlier, scripts are written representations of a visual and auditory medium, therefore screenwriters can't put anything in a script that the screen audience won't see or hear (a comment I gave time and time again as a judge).

This can be technical—e.g. the differences between a spec and shooting script—or it could pertain to the actual story information you can include.

On the technical side, a *spec* script should lead the audience through the story, a *shooting* script includes all the technical verbiage on how to actually *film* the story.

A shooting script might state that the camera zooms in on a string of pearls sitting on a bookshelf, but the audience won't actually see the camera zoom. They see the pearls on the shelf. And that's what goes in the spec script, "A string of pearls rests on the bookshelf," not "The camera zooms in on the string of pearls."

In other words, in a spec script, your description, dialogue, and transitions should do all the camera work for you.

Technical directions aside, proper formatting can go beyond *how* you include information to *the kind* of information you can include.

As a judge I read scripts that were otherwise formatted correctly, but the writer provided a single line of backstory that the screen audience would never receive. Was it helpful to better understand the story? Sure. But I had to treat that line like a piece of evidence struck from the records in court. I had to pretend I'd never read it because, as a judge, I couldn't know anything that the viewing audience wouldn't know.

If the writer provides backstory on the protagonist that would not be available to the screen audience, then it's difficult for a judge to objectively determine how well that character would play on the screen (since the screen audience wouldn't be privy to the same amount of backstory). Will that character be relatable without this knowledge? Will the character seem vulnerable without knowing what led to his/her insecurities? Will the plot still be solid if the audience doesn't know the one little tidbit hidden in the description back on page two?

Conveying exposition in the appropriate format, at the appropriate moment, and in a natural and effective way (all without interrupting the story's pacing) is something any successful writer should master. It's not easy. But it is necessary. And understanding the proper formatting techniques should help.

Bottom line, adhering to proper formatting (making sure your script is spelled and punctuated correctly, using the proper indentations, slug lines, and character cues, etc.) helps ensure your story is *conveyed the way you intended*. While it's important to understand how scripts should be formatted, if you understand *why* scripts require their unique formatting, then you can start to use the formatting tools to tell your story far more accurately and effectively.

Pacing

Pacing is about the moments of a story—the beats. Not just the main plot points (though certainly those apply), but also the tiny moments and all the moments in between.

Pacing affects each scene, each character arc, each plot thread. Pacing affects the emotional and suspenseful highs and lows of the story, the action beats, how and when plot points unfold... Pacing is about *every single beat* of a story: when those beats hit, how long they last, and how they flow into each other.

As a screenwriter, you need to be aware, not just of the pacing of your *story*, but also of the pacing of your *script*.

The two *should* be the same. But that doesn't always mean they are. And it's important for a story to *read* at the same pace as that story will be *viewed*.

As touched on earlier, one page of properly formatted script is about one minute of screen time, which means a 120-page script would be about a two-hour movie. Consequently, if copious amounts of description are written on every page of the script, then it's hard to determine how long the movie will take to play on screen. But just as importantly (or perhaps more so) it's very difficult for a reader to get a sense of a story's pacing *if the description takes longer to read than it would to play out on screen.*

This is one of the reasons why descriptions need to be short (usually four lines or less... preferably less) so that the beats, rhythm, and timing of the description on the page represent the beats, rhythm, and timing of the film or show.

For example, let's say you've crafted twenty lines of beautiful description. Perhaps this description equals just a few seconds of *screen time*. But, at twenty lines, it's going to take more than a few seconds to actually *read* that description.

Now, this isn't to say your description can't be beautifully written. It can! But it needs to also be economically written so it can represent the appropriate pacing. In other words, screenwriters must be selective with their word choices.

A picture is worth a thousand words, right? And with a script you're writing picture after picture on the page—however, you can't use thousands of words to do so (which is a bit of a paradox).

Because of this, it's necessary to select very precise words to convey your intent for the story and to achieve the pacing you want.

For example, you could say, "Sally closes the door behind her," or "Sally raises her chin defiantly, turns, then slams the door behind her," or "Sally starts to leave, but stops. She hesitates with her hand on the doorknob. Then, slowly, she closes the door behind her." In each case, Sally leaves and closes the door, but each description conveys something entirely different about that moment and about Sally—and the pacing of each example is different.

So, if you can identify the *key* word/s you need—the most important characteristics you must convey about an action, a place, or a character—then you've got a better chance at achieving and conveying both your intended story and intended pacing. (Everything else will be left in the hands of the production designers, the costume designers, the set decorators, the cinematographers, the director, the actors... everyone involved whose job it is to tell the story in the most effective way possible. Because, at the end of the day, while these individuals may not be writers, *they are all storytellers*.)

In addition to being selective about the words you use in your script, you can be selective about the scenes you include, too. Transitions are one of my favorite screenwriting tools because, when used effectively, transitions can help the pacing and execution of your story.

How scenes lead out of and into each other greatly influence the pacing and intent of the moment. Do the scenes flow naturally? Do you intend for the scene change to be abrupt? Maybe you want that missed beat as a comedic moment. If so, be aware of how your script's transitions will play to the reader because how you use transitions will lead the reader (or viewer) to certain conclusions.

For example, suppose you end a scene with James on the phone saying, "It's all set, Sarah. I'm leaving right now and will meet you at the park." Then James hangs up the phone and grabs his keys. It *seems* like the next scene should be James and Sarah at the park. For example:

```
EXT.  PARK – DAY
```

Followed by the description:

```
James and Sarah stand under a willow tree.
```

In this case, the reader's eyes would probably glide right over that scene heading in an almost automatic way—and that's okay because you led the reader there.

Moreover, you didn't need to show James and Sarah traveling to the park. You didn't need to show a sign beside them that reads "State Park." In fact, you could probably get away with James' dialogue being, "It's all set, Sarah. I'm leaving now."

However, if James says, "It's all set, Sarah. I'm leaving right now and will meet you at the park," and the next scene heading reads:

```
INT. HOSPITAL – DAY
```

Followed by the description:

```
James on a gurney, unconscious.
```

Now the reader is wondering, "What happened on the way to the park!?" And maybe that's the response you want. But if it isn't, then you have a problem to fix.

Knowing how transitions affect your story and what they will cause your audience to infer is crucial because *what you don't say in a script is often just as important as what you do say.*

So once you understand how to use transitions, you can use them to your story's advantage.

Lastly, I want to clarify that *pacing* and *length* are not the same.

This was one of the best insights I learned about writing, and I learned it from watching filmmaker commentaries about deleted scenes.

You see, initially I didn't understand why directors would cut perfectly beautiful scenes from movies because "the movie was too long." At two hours, did it really matter if there was an extra 30 seconds of film? What I came to realize was that the *length* of the film wasn't usually (or solely) the issue. It was the *pacing* of the film. And, yes, 30 seconds can be a huge deal when it comes to pacing. Even two seconds can affect pacing! Consider comedy: timing is everything, right? So, if the pacing of a joke is off, it could affect the entire joke, possibly the entire scene. Maybe even the entire plot point.

Pacing affects every story, no matter the genre. If it's a drama, then the pacing can affect the emotional impact of a moment, a scene, or the entire story.

Achieving the right pacing is a challenge—otherwise directors wouldn't film beautiful scenes that later end up on the cutting room floor because the scene hurt the pacing.

You can have a script that comes in at a brisk 85 pages, but if the pacing is wrong it can feel like 200 pages. Likewise, you can have a 135-page script that moves so quickly it feels like it's only 50 pages. I'm not saying that the *story* has to be sparse, or that you have to chip away at the complexity of your characters, but the moments have to fall into each other so that the pacing moves seamlessly and fluidly through the story. The better the pacing, the more the reader will want to keep reading, and the more engaged in the story he/she will become.

Remember, your script is a written representation of how you envision your story playing out on the screen. Therefore, the story should come at the *reader* in the same way it would come at the *viewing audience*—the same rhythm, the same pacing, the same focus. And your job as the screenwriter is to determine the beats of your *story*, and then accurately convert those beats to the *page*.

So, if your script doesn't score well in the pacing criterion, you may need to analyze if it's an issue with the pacing of the story, the pacing of the script, or both.

Character

A script is largely about the characters that inhabit the story.

For this criterion, judges might ask: Are the characters interesting? Are they unique from one another? Are they unique from other stories? Do the characters' actions fit their personalities? Do the characters' actions progress the story? Are their goals clearly defined? Does the judge care about the characters? Do the characters change or grow throughout the story? Do the characters' actions tell the reader about who they are (especially since writers are limited on the exposition they can use to do so)?

Are the characters engaging (do you want to know more about them) even if they aren't likeable? Does the judge feel invested in the characters and want to know what happens to them? Are both the protagonist *and* antagonist multi-layered? Do the supporting characters have their own arcs, goals, and moments to shine without taking away from the protagonist's moment to shine?

Do all the characters fit the story and the world the writer's placed them in? If the script is a spec for an existing series, are the characters and their actions consistent with what the series already developed? If the script is a pilot for a *new* series, are the characters interesting enough that a viewer would want to invest several episodes or seasons with them?

I admit, the degree to which someone connects with a character can be fairly subjective. But a competition's judging criteria can guide judges to consider certain objective points in order to more fairly evaluate characters.

Dialogue

Dialogue refers to the words spoken by the characters in your story.

Typically, judges want characters' voices to be unique from each other. A good check for this is to read the dialogue in your script *without* reading the corresponding character cue names and see if you can determine who is speaking just by the word choices, phrasing, and pacing of the dialogue.

Some questions judges might ask relative to the dialogue

criterion are: Is the dialogue appropriate to each character? Does the dialogue help propel the story forward, or is there superfluous dialogue that doesn't propel the story or convey anything about the characters? Are there too many long chunks of dialogue? Too many speeches? Is each character's dialogue and voice consistent throughout the story? Does the dialogue fit both the character and his/her world? Are the word choices appropriate to the character's age, history, location, era? If, for example, the script is an historical script then the characters shouldn't use modern slang (unless, of course, there's a reason for the contradiction). Does the character's style of speaking make sense for his/her backstory? Maybe one character is always sarcastic. What would happen if that character finally said what he/she actually meant? How would the writer convey that? What would it say about that character at that moment in the story?

Judges often comment that they do not want a character to say *exactly* what he/she means, wants or feels since rarely in real life do people come right out and say what they're thinking or feeling. With this in mind, how natural is the dialogue in your script? How well does the dialogue convey a point, an emotion, or a thought, without coming right out and *literally* saying it?

Commercial Potential

It costs money to make films, television shows, digital series, mini-series, etc. And part of this cost includes paying you, the writer. So, in order to continue to make films, shows, etc., the money invested in them must yield profits. That means audiences have to buy movie tickets, or rent Blu-rays, or sign-up for streaming subscriptions, etc. So, (unless your film project is self-funded) if you expect to get paid, then someone else needs to buy what you've created. For that reason alone, it is perfectly acceptable for a competition to judge your script based on the perception of its commercial potential.

However...

Some films and shows are critically outstanding, even if they don't have high commercial appeal. Because of this, I don't believe the *quality* of a script should be judged at a lesser standard because it might have a smaller audience appeal or appeals to a niche market.

Moreover, films and shows sometimes become commercial hits that no one, even film professionals, expected to garner wide audience appeal. So, having commercial appeal as a judging criterion when even industry professionals can't always predict commercial success might not be the most accurate way to judge a script.

That being said, when you submit your script to agents, managers, and producers, they will undoubtedly evaluate your script's commercial potential. So if a competition is trying to discover those scripts that have the best chance of being produced, then adding a commercial potential judging criterion makes sense.

Bottom line, whether or not commercial potential is a judging criterion used by the competition you enter, it's important for screenwriters to have their pulse on what audiences will pay to see. And being aware of the commercial appeal of the story you've written can be very helpful in determining which competitions to enter (and, down the road, which agents, managers, or producers to query).

Voice/Style/Tone

When "voice" is a judging criterion, typically the competition is referring to the *voice of the writer*.

It's difficult to get a solid definition of voice. Voice is rather like "the 'it' factor"—hard to define, but noticeable when it's there (or when it's not).

In general, voice is made up of a writer's writing style: the tone he/she uses for the story, the overall *feel* of the story, the pacing of the story, and story aspects the writer focuses on and emphasizes.

Some questions that judges might ask relative to this criterion might be: What is *this writer's* overall style of writing? Are descriptions in full sentences or do they cut to the chase? Is the style succinct? Fluid? Are descriptions fluid overall but abrupt during action sequences? Is the style *consistent* throughout the script (or does the writer constantly and arbitrarily switch styles)? If the style changes, is there a reason (relative to the story) for the change? Is there an overall tone to the story? Does that tone match the story written? And is that tone consistent from start to finish? If not, is there a reason for the change?

Whatever style you write, will the reader's eyes flow easily through the pages or will the reader feel jarred from the story again and again?

For example, have you ever started a script, a film, or a book then so many pages or minutes into the story suddenly feel like it is a totally *different* story? This could be an issue with the plot (the story itself switches direction to something unrelated to the setup), or the structure (the setup needs to be re-written to focus on the main threads of the story), *or* it could be an issue with the *tone* (the plot and structure are consistent, but the story *feels* different). Said another way: If the *focus* of the story changes, it's probably an issue with plot or structure. If the story *feels* different, it's probably an issue with tone.

Whatever voice, style, and tone you use, it should match the story you've written, it should cinematically and effectively convey the story, its feel, and its mood.

If the voice feels fresh and unique, all the better.

Theme

Theme is the message, or moral, of your story. Different than the concept, the theme is the "point" that the concept and plot end up conveying to the audience.

Theme can be conveyed through plot, dialogue, and visual elements. Ideally, the concept, plot, and theme should support each other. The plot should embody the concept, and the theme should be revealed through the plot (rather than the writer needing to come right out and say it).

Originality

What elements of your story are original: The concept? The plot? The structure? The characters? All of it?

Competitions often want their judges to give a positive ranking to a story that is original—an entirely new plot, a retold story with a twist, or a fresh take on an old idea. But exactly how competitions assess originality is unique to each competition.

Overall

Sometimes competitions have an "overall" judging criterion. In other words, what was the judge's *overall impression* of the script? What did the judge take away from your story? Was the judge emotionally moved? Did the judge want to keep reading to find out how the story ended? Did the judge feel invested in the story, the plot, and the characters? Even if the script had flaws, did the judge identify something special about the story that made it stand out?

Criteria Summary

Not every competition will use the preceding judging criteria. Moreover, each competition usually includes criteria that are more unique (e.g. conflict or casting potential). So, identify what each competition uses for their judging criteria so that you can select competitions that are more likely to reward the script you've written.

Also remember: judges use criteria to evaluate the story that's on the page. So it's up to the writer to not only create a convincing world and plot filled with compelling characters, but to make sure all of that is accurately and effectively represented *within the pages of the script.*

5

The Ranking Process

Once a judge reads a script and evaluates its strengths and weaknesses, the judge needs a way to quantify those evaluations so that the script can be ranked in the competition.

In my experience, four types of quantifiers are used by competitions to rank scripts. This doesn't mean there aren't other quantifiers (and not all competitions post which ones they use), but these four quantifiers appear to be the most common:

1. Scores
2. Recommendations
3. Comments
4. Discussions

I'll discuss each quantifier in this chapter, but first know that some competitions use only one type of quantifier for the entire judging process. Other competitions use multiple quantifiers (either within a round, or different quantifiers for different rounds).

For example, while one competition might use scores to rank scripts throughout the entire competition, another competition might use scores for the first two rounds and then use a combination of scores and discussion for the final round.

Scores

When a competition uses scores to rank scripts, it is asking judges to convert script evaluations into numeric ranks. Usually this happens in one of two ways.

1. The judge assigns the script a single *overall* score. For example, a competition might utilize a 1 to 10 scale: "1" means the script needs copious amounts of work, and "10" means the script is perfect.

2. The judge scores the script per judging criterion, then totals those numbers for the script's final score. For example:

   Plot = 9
   Structure = 8
   Characters = 8
   Dialogue = 7
   Presentation = 10
   TOTAL = 42 out of 50

When your script is scored per judging criterion, it makes it easy to see at a glance where your script excels and where it needs work. Moreover, knowing your script's total score is one of the easiest ways to determine where your script stacked up against the competition (which I'll discuss further in "Determining Advancement" in Chapter 6).

The slight hiccup, however, is that it's rare for competitions to actually release your script's competition score.

As I write this, the Academy Nicholl Fellowships in Screenwriting (Nicholl) comes close. If your script scores 60 or higher then Nicholl will provide you with the *type* of score your script received. So, while you won't receive your script's actual score, you'll have an approximate idea of how each judge ranked your script. For example, according to a 2015 Nicholl Facebook post: If your script received a "high-score" or "strong positive score" then that script scored 80 or more. A "positive score" meant a score of 60-79. This information becomes even more useful if you can find the percentage of scripts that received a score similar to the one assigned to your script (as well as the percentage of scripts that scored higher and lower).

Some competitions only provide your script's score if you purchase a written critique (and if that critique is written by your script's competition judge). For example, if (in conjunction with your competition entry) you purchase Judge's Feedback from the PAGE International Screenwriting Awards (PAGE), then you will receive a written critique from your *first round judge* in the competition. That critique will include the actual competition scores the judge assigned your script (broken down by judging criterion). If you have this score, you'll be better able to determine where your script ranked relative to the other entries that year.

Not all critiques written by competition judges will include scores. Moreover, some competitions allow you to purchase written critiques in conjunction with your competition entry—but those critiques will not be written by your script's competition judge (even if scores are included with your critique, it does not necessarily mean the scores were the ones your script received in the competition). This doesn't mean one type of critique is better or worse than another. But it's important to read about the critique offered to ensure you understand what you are purchasing. (I'll discuss critiques further in Section III).

So why are scripts' competition scores rarely released?

Many competitions state that the reason they won't release scores is because scores alone don't provide writers with enough information.

I do understand this point of view—especially when the script only receives a single, overall score. If your script scores a 50 out of 100 then you know your script needs a lot of work, but you won't know *which* areas need work. Maybe your plot and structure need fixing but your characters are great. But without that insight you might decide to change your characters and leave your plot as written.

However, when a score is broken down *by criterion*, it helps to identify your script's strengths and weaknesses. This is especially useful if you receive scores from multiple judges (and, even better, from multiple competitions). For example, let's say your script consistently scores a 5 out of 10 for characters and a 9 out of 10 for every other criterion. This gives you a pretty clear idea that you need to focus on rewriting your characters to get your script to the next level.

But, even if you find that your characters need work, is that awareness enough? Will you be able to identify the exact problems and know *how* to improve your characters? If not, you might benefit from further guidance (like written critiques).

So, yes, I fully understand why competitions are hesitant to release script scores. But I also think that knowing how your script ranks (especially per criterion) can elevate the benefit you receive from the competition process, if you know what to do with the information.

Recommendations

Judges also rank scripts by assigning recommendations.

A judge might have two ranking options: the script should advance in the competition, or the script should *not* advance in the competition.

Or a judge might have multiple ranking options, such as recommending the script advance to the next round but no further, recommending the script advance to the semifinals, recommending the script be considered for the win, or recommending the script be eliminated from the competition.

Comments

Judges are often required to write comments about the scripts they read. These comments may or may not be used to rank scripts.

Sometimes the comments (or notes) are used by a competition's organizers to keep tabs on their judges to help ensure the rankings assigned by each judge are consistent with the judge's comments and the competition's judging criteria.

But sometimes comments are used as part of the ranking process.

It's unusual for a competition to use *only* comments to rank scripts. Instead, it's more likely that the competition will use judges' comments along with other ranking quantifiers.

For example, in some cases a judge might submit a score as well as comments. Those scores and comments might both be taken into consideration when determining whether a script should advance or not.

In other cases, final round judges might read and evaluate the finalists' scripts, but *also* read the comments from those scripts' previous judges and take those comments into consideration when determining which script/s should win.

Discussion

Advancement is sometimes determined when judges get together and talk about the scripts comprising that round of competition. The judges then decide amongst themselves which scripts deserve to advance.

This usually only happens during the final round of competition when the judges are selecting the winner/s. However, discussion might not be the *only* factor in determining the winning scripts. Judges might also consider the scripts' previous scores, recommendations, and/or comments.

6

The Advancement Process

I vividly remember receiving a phone call from AFF to inform me that my script had advanced to the semifinals in the sci-fi genre. I was thrilled! I was shaking with excitement. But I didn't actually realize how special this achievement was. The AFF representative on the phone must have suspected my ignorance because he tried very kindly to convey to me just how rare it was to reach the semifinals at AFF.

You see, my script had already placed in other competitions—fairly consistently making it to the quarterfinals (and, don't get me wrong, every time one of my scripts makes it to the quarterfinals in any competition I'm delighted!). But, at that moment on the phone, I didn't really know what being an AFF semifinalist meant. At best, I thought it meant my script had reached the top 10% or 15% of sci-fi entries.

It wasn't until I got off the phone and reviewed AFF's competition information that I realized making the semifinals at AFF meant I'd placed in the top 2% of sci-fi entries. *Top 2%!* I was floored! I still get chills when I remember that moment. And to top that off, the judges who had selected my script for that top 2% were working in the film industry, and that felt very validating.

So, mea culpa AFF. If only AFF's rep heard me an hour after I'd hung up the phone. Of course, it's very possible he *did* hear me shout with joy even though he was halfway across the country.

My point is, when you succeed, I want you to be able to fully understand and enjoy the moment. And to do that, you have to understand not only the competition's judging process, but also how the competition advances scripts.

By understanding the judging and advancement process you'll have greater insight into what it took for your script to be advanced (or eliminated) and how many judges it took to make that decision. That information can help give you a better idea of how much work your script needs, and which competitions favorably rank your type of script.

The way in which competitions determine which scripts advance, as well as the *number* of scripts that advance, varies significantly across competitions (and also from round to round *within* a competition). But, typically, there are two parts to the advancement process:

1. The *threshold* a script must reach in order to advance in the competition.

2. The *number* of judges' ranks required to determine advancement.

Advancement Thresholds and Qualifiers

To advance scripts, competitions have to set **advancement thresholds** for each round of competition—the *rank* a script must achieve in order to advance.

In my experience, three types of thresholds are used to advance scripts:

1. Qualifying Rank

2. Qualifying Percentage

3. Qualifying Number

Qualifying Rank

Competitions that use a qualifying rank advance scripts that receive a predetermined rank (or higher) *regardless of the ranks received by the other scripts in the competition.*

For example, as I write this, in order to advance to the second round of competition at PAGE, a script must receive a first round score of 60 or higher. Similarly, to advance to the second round at Nicholl, a script typically needs a score of 80 or higher from at least one judge.

Scriptapalooza's International Screenplay Competition uses a qualifying rank in their first round of competition since any script that receives a *recommendation for advancement* from the script's first round judge will advance to the second round, regardless of how many other scripts receive advancement recommendations.

Qualifying Percentage

Competitions use a *qualifying percentage* when they advance scripts that rank in the top *predetermined percent of rankings* (e.g. top 10%). In this case, a script's advancement *will* be affected by the ranks given to the other scripts in the competition.

For example, let's say you enter the same script in the same competition for two consecutive years. This competition advances the top scoring 10% of scripts to their second round of judging. Both years your script scores 90 out of 100. The first year, 10% of scripts receive a score of 85 or higher. This means your script would advance that year. However, the following year 10% of scripts receive a score of 93 or higher. This means your script would *not* advance that year, even though it received the same score as the previous year.

The percentile of scripts that are allowed to advance varies substantially across competitions—and from round to round within a competition. For example, as I write this, the top scoring 10% of scripts at PAGE advance to the quarterfinals. At ScreenCraft's Sci-Fi and Fantasy Contest, the top scoring 25% of scripts advance to the *quarterfinals* (and the top scoring 10% advance to the *semifinals)*.

And this brings me to an important point. When a competition mentions an advancing percentage (e.g. quarterfinalists make up the top 25%) the percentage is typically calculated based on the number of *total* entries, not the number of scripts judged during that round.

So, let's say a competition has four rounds of judging:

- The first round (all entries are read).
- The quarterfinal round (representing the top 25% of entries).
- The semifinal round (representing the top 10% of entries).
- The final round (representing the top 5% of entries).

If that competition received 10,000 entries, the number of scripts judged per round would be:

- The first round: 10,000 scripts.
- The quarterfinal round: 2,500 scripts.
- The semifinal round: 1,000 scripts.
- The final round: 500 scripts.

However, if the advancing percentages were based on the number of scripts *per round* (not the total entries) then the numbers would be:

- The first round: 10,000 scripts.
- The quarterfinal round: 2,500 scripts (since this first advancement is still based on the total entries).
- The semifinal round: 250 scripts (10% of 2,500).
- The final round: 12-13 scripts (5% of 250).

Finally, if a competition uses format, genre or category-specific judging, then the advancing percentages may be based on the total entries *or* the entries per format/genre/category.

Qualifying Number

A competition uses a qualifying number when *a set number of scripts advance*, regardless of how many scripts are entered in a competition (e.g. the top ranking 100 scripts, or the top ranking 5 scripts).

Like the qualifying percentage, when a competition advances scripts using the qualifying number threshold, whether your script advances or not *will* be affected by the ranks the rest of the scripts receive in the competition.

For example, as I write this, the Nashville Film Festival Screenwriting Competition advances three scripts (per genre) to the final round, regardless of the number of total entries. And PAGE (again, regardless of the number of total entries) advances the top 25 scripts to their semifinal round per format/genre/category, and advances 10 scripts to their final round per format/genre/category.

Round Variations

Many competitions apply different advancement thresholds for different rounds of competition. For example, a competition might:

- Advance scripts that score 70 or higher to their quarterfinal round (qualifying rank).
- Advance the top scoring 10 *percent* of scripts to their semifinal round (qualifying percentage).
- Advance the top *5 scripts* to their final round (qualifying number).

Format, Genre or Category-Specific Thresholds

I want to point out a few things about competitions that use format, genre and/or category-specific judging relative to advancement thresholds.

When competitions use a qualifying rank to advance scripts, whether or not the competition advances scripts per format/genre/category would not affect the script's potential for advancement because a script advances if it receives a high enough rank regardless of the ranks received by other scripts.

However, if competitions advance scripts using a qualifying percentage or qualifying number, then it becomes important to know if those advancements are per format/genre/category or based on the total number of entries.

Whether advancements are made per format/genre/category or not depends on the individual competition—and sometimes the round *within* a competition. For example, a competition might advance all scripts that receive a score of 70 or higher to the quarterfinals (regardless of format/genre/category) but advance the top scoring 10 scripts *per* format/genre/category to the semifinals.

Summary

So, which advancement threshold is best: qualifying rank, qualifying percentage, or qualifying number? Of the three types, I prefer the qualifying rank because it means my script advanced (or not) based on its own merits, regardless of the number or quality of scripts entered that year.

Multiple Judges and Ranks

Knowing the number of judges it took to advance (or eliminate) my script provides me with a better understanding of how my script was received and by how many individuals. For example, did only one judge deem my script worthy of advancement? Or did three judges think my script should advance? Or did one judge think my script should advance, but another judge thought my script should be eliminated?

Whatever the result, I find the information helpful.

However, while some competitions clearly explain the number of judges they require to rank a script before determining advancement, other competitions don't explain this process at all, and some explain the process used for early rounds of competition, but not later rounds (or vice versa).

It's also important to note that the *number of judges* who read your script does not necessarily equal the *number of rounds* your script advanced through. This is because it's fairly common for competitions to require each script to be read and ranked by more than one judge *per round of competition*. Therefore, a script can end up with multiple ranks when:

- The script is read and ranked by *more than one judge per round of competition*.

And/or:

- The script *advances in the competition* resulting in the script being read and ranked by a new judge (or judges).

When scripts acquire multiple ranks, competitions typically handle it in one of the following ways:

- ***Total***. All of a script's ranks are combined and the total determines if the script advances. For example, if a script receives three scores (50, 75, and 100), then 225 would be the rank used to determine if the script advances or not.

- ***Average***. All of a script's ranks are compiled, and the average determines if the script advances. For example, if a script receives the scores 50, 75, and 100, then the average (75) would be the rank used to determine if the script advances or not.

- ***Removing the Lows***. The lowest of a script's rank/s is/are removed and the total or average of the remaining ranks determines if the script advances. For example, if a script receives the scores 50, 75, and 100, then either: 1) the highest score (100) is used to determine if the script advances; or 2) the lowest score (50) is removed and the remaining two scores (75 and 100) would be the ranks used to determine if the script advances—either by totaling the two scores (175) or using the average of those two scores (87.5).

- ***Combinations***. A competition might use a combination of the preceding methods. For example, a competition might judge every entry twice and

> score scripts on a 1 to 100 scale. Then, to advance to the second round, a script might need *either* a score of 85 or higher from at least *one* judge *or* a *combined* score of 160 from *two* judges.

I like the method of removing the lowest rank/s because when a script is read by a judge who (for whatever reason) doesn't connect with the story, then that judge's rank doesn't follow the script during the entire competition.

I should mention that the number of judges who must read your script *per round* could be dependent on the rank assigned by the script's first judge in that round. For example, a competition might require only one judge to *advance* a script but require two judges to *eliminate* a script. So, if the first judge gives your script an advancing rank, then the script advances to the next round of competition having only been judged once. If the first judge does *not* give your script an advancing rank then your script must be read by a second judge. If that second judge gives your script an advancing rank, then the script advances. But if the second judge *doesn't* give your script an advancing rank, then your script would be eliminated from the competition. In either case, this would only be one round of competition—because *the script was only advanced or eliminated once*.

Finally, as scripts advance they acquire one or more ranks from *each* round of competition. Depending on the competition's advancement process, a script advances based on *either* the ranks the script receives *per round* (a script's rank, in essence, starts over with each round) or *cumulatively* (the ranks from current *and* previous rounds are used to determine advancement).

Competition Rounds and Advancement Tiers

A **competition round** is a portion of a competition in which scripts are read, evaluated, and ranked. Those rankings (or those rankings in addition to the script's rankings received in previous rounds) determine which scripts advance in the competition and which scripts are eliminated. Once those advancements and eliminations occur, the next round begins.

This seems pretty straight-forward at first. And knowing how many rounds your script advanced through can be helpful in determining the strength of your script. But here's the thing: competitions don't always release the results of *every round of competition*. While some competitions do provide entrants with personal notifications that tell each entrant how many rounds his/her script advanced through, most competitions only release results associated with **advancement tiers**.

An advancement tier is a round of competition in which the competition publicly announces the scripts that reach that specific round. Because of this, each advancement tier might consist of *multiple rounds of competition* that culminate in a single advancement tier.

For example, a script might go through three rounds of judging and advancements to reach the quarterfinal advancement tier. So, while a competition might publicly announce which scripts reach the quarterfinals, they might not release which scripts advanced through the first, second and third rounds. In this case, if your script does not make the quarterfinals, you won't know how close it came to doing so. Was your script eliminated after the first round of competition or did it make it to the third round before it got cut?

Most competitions have four advancement tiers. The most common (in order of advancement) are:

- Quarterfinals
- Semifinals

- Finals
- Winners

While these are the most common terms, you may come across other terms (AFF uses the term "Second Rounders" in lieu of "quarterfinals") and/or *additional tiers* (Nicholl has a "Top 50 Screenplays" list that's comprised of high-scoring scripts from the semifinals, finals and winners).

An advancement tier also represents the placement your script achieved in the competition. For example, your script *reached* the quarterfinal round but *placed* as a quarterfinalist.

The number or percentage of scripts that make up advancement tiers varies substantially from one competition to another. Therefore, understanding what a competition's advancement tiers represent is incredibly important when you're trying to determine:

1. How your script stacks up against the competition.

2. Which placements are worthy of inclusion in your queries and pitches.

3. Which placements are likely to garner interest from the film industry.

For example, placing as a *semifinalist* in a competition where the semifinalists represent the top 15% of entries likely won't garner as much interest from the industry as placing as a *quarterfinalist* in a competition where the quarterfinalists represent the top 5% of entries (provided, of course, that both competitions are equally known and respected).

That said, if your script isn't at top 5% status, entering competitions that advance a larger percentage of scripts to initial tiers (or competitions that provide entrants with the number of rounds their scripts advanced through) will give you a better idea of where your script stacks up against the competition (but more on this in Chapter 8 and Section V).

Determining Advancement

Even if a competition doesn't notify entrants or publicly announce the results of all rounds of competition, you can sometimes determine how many rounds of competition your script survived by gathering other information.

One way to do this is by using the *rank* your script received (e.g. If the competition requires a score of 75 or more to advance to the second round of judging and your script scored an 82, then your script advanced). Or you might be able to use the *number of judges or critiques* your script received to determine how far your script advanced (e.g. If scripts are judged only once per round and you receive critiques from three judges, then your script advanced through three rounds).

Many competitions, however, do not provide enough information for you to determine exactly how far your script advanced. But some do if you know what to look for. I'll use the initial rounds of the PAGE competition as an example.

PAGE's quarterfinal round is made up of the top scoring 10% of entries. To reach the quarterfinal round, a script must survive *two* rounds of judging. However, PAGE only announces those scripts that advance to the quarterfinals—not the scripts that make it to the second round of judging.

So, if your script *does* make the quarterfinals, great! You know that your script scored in the top 10%. But if your script did *not* make the quarterfinals, you won't know if your script scored in the top 11% and barely missed out on the quarterfinals, or if it scored in the bottom 3% and didn't make it to the second round of judging.

But, all is not lost!

Even though PAGE doesn't automatically release scores, you can purchase PAGE's Judge's Feedback in conjunction with your competition entry. That Feedback is a critique written *by your script's first round judge*, and it includes the score he/she gave your script (broken down per judging criteria no less).

Not only do these scores give you a better idea of the strengths and weaknesses of your script relative to the judging criteria, but the total score gives you a better idea where among the competition your script ranked because to reach PAGE's second round of judging, a script needs a score of 60 or higher. And since PAGE states that approximately 25% of entries advance to the second round, if you have your first round score, you'll know if your script made that top 25% or not.

Knowing whether your script scores in the top 25% versus the top 10% might not sound like a huge difference, however, based on my experience, a script that consistently ranks in the top 25% of competitions (but not higher) is of an entirely different quality than a script that consistently reaches the top 10%—but more on this in Section V.

Even if you advance, PAGE's Judge's Feedback only entitles you to one written critique (and thus one judge's scores). But the score from your first round judge will give you an idea of how your *second* round judge scored your script. If the first round judge gave your script a high score but you still didn't make the quarterfinals, then the second judge must have scored your script significantly lower because the combined score wasn't enough to make the top 10%.

Before moving on to the next portion of this chapter, I want to mention that—in addition to helping you determine the quality of your script—knowing how far your script advanced in a competition can sometimes help you determine the *credentials of the judges who read your script*. This is because competitions often post the *types* of credentials their judges have *per round of competition*. So if you know which rounds your script was judged in, you can get an idea as to the film experience of the judges who chose to advance (or eliminate) your script.

Having your script eliminated by a fellow aspiring screenwriter might not carry as much weight as an elimination by a major film producer. Or, having your script *advanced* by a major producer might make you feel a little more validated than being advanced by a fellow aspiring writer.

This isn't to say that reasonable opinions can't come from anyone, but knowing the background of the person making decisions about your script can help when you're trying to decide how much weight to put on an advancement/elimination (as well as any critiques you receive, but that's discussed in Section III).

Announcements and Notifications

As stated earlier, some competitions provide entrants with personalized notifications that inform each entrant how many rounds his/her script advanced through. But this is rare. Publicly announcing the results of advancement tiers is more common. However, while many competitions publicly announce the results of multiple advancement tiers, some competitions only announce the results of a few tiers. For example, the Nashville Film Festival Screenwriting Competition announces which scripts make the semifinals and above. The Sun Valley Film Festival High Scribe Screenplay Competition announces finalists and winners.

More importantly, if a competition announces which scripts reach which advancement tiers but does not *also* announce the *total number of scripts entered* and the number and/or percentage of scripts each advancement tier represents, then it can still be difficult to determine how your script stacked up against the other entries. Having your script selected as one of the top ten finalists is a great feeling! But knowing whether it made the top ten out of 200 entries versus 7,000 entries would give you more insight.

Does this mean these types of competitions are better or worse than others? Not at all. However, it *does* mean that you won't get much insight into how your script ranked *unless* it wins or places highly, and that's not very helpful when you're trying to determine how much rewriting your script requires. (Of course, if the competition provides written critiques, then you can use those to glean more information.) While winning these types of competitions might still help advance your career, if your goal is to get a better understanding as to the quality of your script, these competitions probably aren't your best investment.

To help determine if a competition announces multiple advancement tiers, check their announcement dates. If the competition announces various tiers of advancement, they will likely list multiple announcement dates (and the advancement tier that corresponds with each date). For example: semifinalists will be announced on January 1st, finalists will be announced on February 1st.

You could also try to find the competition's **advancement announcements** from previous years. Search their website, social media pages, or try an Internet search like "Script Pipeline Screenwriting Competition 2017 Finalists." If you find these announcements, you can see which tiers were announced and also if the competition provided information regarding the total number of entries received that year and/or the percentage of entries the advancement tier represented (e.g. top 25%).

It's worth noting that even if the competition doesn't make this information publicly available, they may provide it in notification emails to the entrants. However, you might not be able to find out if that's the case prior to entering the competition.

7

The Competition Round Template

I created three templates that I use for my competition research and record keeping. I am making them available to you in this book. Feel free to use them as presented, or you're welcome to customize them to fit your needs.

I'll discuss templates again in Section VII, but I want to explain the Competition Round Template here since it helps illustrate and summarize the topics covered in the previous chapters.

The Competition Round Template is designed to help you identify and organize a competition's judging and advancement process, which should help you determine which competitions are a good fit for you and your script.

If you enter the competition, the completed template makes it easier to figure out how far your script advanced in the competition and the judging process involved (since this can vary greatly among competitions).

For example, maybe your script advanced to the semifinals in one competition but only the quarterfinals in another—but maybe it took *two* judges' ranks to make the first competition's semifinals, but *five* judges to give your script an advancing rank to reach the quarterfinals of the second competition.

You'll need to complete the Competition Round Template per *round* per *competition*. However, be aware that most competitions won't provide all the information necessary to comprehensively complete the template. But some do come close. For example, both PAGE and Nicholl provide a good amount of explanation regarding their judging and advancement process. But many competitions aren't this thorough, often explaining how scripts are judged and advanced for initial rounds of competition, but not for later rounds (or vice versa). And some competitions don't explain their judging/advancement process at all.

Nevertheless, by completing the template as thoroughly as possible, you can better identify the competitions that provide the most information about how scripts are ranked, and (for the competitions that you enter) which competitions most consistently reward your type of writing.

It should also be noted that some of the information required to complete the Competition Round Template won't be available until *after* the competition closes for entries and/or ends. For example, you won't be able to record the number of total entries the competition receives until the competition closes for entries and releases the final count.

Additionally, competitions might change their judging or advancement procedures from year to year. By keeping records, I have found that I can easily update my completed template to reflect a competition's process for the current year *and*, just as importantly, I can look back at the process used for my entries in prior years.

To make this easier, I suggest you file your completed Competition Round Template by *competition*, by *year*, and/or by *script* (and script version). This way you can easily reference the template in the future.

On the following page is a Competition Round Template completed for the first round of a fictionalized competition: "The 2020 Mock Screenplay Contest." While the competition is fabricated, I've tried to keep the information similar to what you'll likely encounter when researching real competitions.

I've only included a completed template for *one* round of the competition here, but Section VII includes template entries for all five rounds of this mock competition. If you like, you can skip ahead to those pages now so you can see how you might record multiple rounds of a competition.

The Competition Round Template Example

Part A

Competition Name:	The 2020 Mock Screenplay Contest
Competition Year:	2020

Part B

Round	1 of 5
Round Terminology	Preliminary Round
Judge Credentials	Professional Script Readers
What is Judged	All entries in their entirety
Number of Judges	One
Ranking Quantifier	Numerical Scores
Cumulative Rank	N.A.
Advancement Threshold	Scripts that score 60 or higher

Part C

Total Entries	6200
Judged this Round	6200 (100% of entries)
Number that Advance	1315
Percent that Advance	21% of all entries

Part D

1st Genre

Genre Entered	Drama
Total Genre Entries	1873
Judged this Round	1873 (100% of drama entries)
Number that Advance	379
Percent that Advance	20% of all drama entries

2nd Genre

Genre Entered	Sci-Fi
Total Genre Entries	658
Judged this Round	658 (100% of sci-fi entries)
Number that Advance	127
Percent that Advance	19% of all sci-fi entries

Part E

Script Entered	The Next Best Screenplay, version 18.9
My Results, Drama	Advanced
My Results, Sci-Fi	Advanced

The Competition Round Template Explained

What follows is a brief explanation of the fields used in the Competition Round template.

Part A

Part A exists so you can easily reference your completed templates by competition name and competition year.

Competition Name. Record the *official* name of the competition. For example, rather than record "AFF", instead record "The Twenty-Fifth Annual Austin Film Festival Screenplay & Teleplay Competition."

By accurately listing the competition's official name in your records, if you want to reference a win/placement in a query or pitch, you'll have the proper data recorded.

Competition Year. This is not necessarily the year you entered the competition.

Most competitions occur annually, so to differentiate they often include the year as part of the competition name. For example, the 2018 Academy Nicholl Fellowships in Screenwriting, or Final Draft®'s 2018 Big Break® Screenwriting Contest.

Many competitions actually take place over two calendar years. A competition might open for entries in December of 2018 and announce results in July of 2019. So the year the competition references in their name is either the year the competition opens for entries or the year the competition announces the winners.

Other competitions don't use the calendar year for reference, instead referencing the number of years the competition has been running (e.g. The Twenty-Fifth Annual Austin Film Festival Screenwriting and Teleplay Competition).

Part B

This portion of the template includes fields for round data and information about the competition's judging/advancement process.

Round. Once you've determined the number of rounds the competition uses, you can use this field to record that total number, along with the round number specific to the individual template entry (e.g. Round 1 of 5). Remember, the total number of rounds may differ from the number of advancement tiers.

Round Terminology. In this field record the *terminology* the competition uses to refer to the corresponding round. For example, your "Round 1 of 5" will probably be called the Preliminary Round or the First Round by the competition. But your "Round 2 of 5" might *also* be called the Preliminary Round or First Round since the competition might use two *rounds* of competition prior to the advancement tier.

Judge Credentials. In this field record the credentials (if known) of the judges for this round. Later, if you happen to learn the credentials of your *actual* judge, include those credentials here. For example:

Judge Credentials	Professional Script Readers.
vs.	
Judge Credentials	My Judge: Script Reader at *Example Productions*

You probably won't know the credentials of your specific judge *unless* you order a critique written by your script's competition judge (and even then it's rare to get specific credentials).

What is Judged. Use this field to record the number (or percent) of scripts judged during this round. If it's the first round, it should be all entries. If it's the finals, it should reflect the number/percent of scripts that advanced to the final round (e.g. the top 5% of all entries or the top 10 scripts per genre).

If you come across a competition that does not read scripts in their entirety, you may choose to denote that in this field of the template. For example:

What is Judged	All entries in their entirety.
vs.	
What is Judged	All entries (a judge may eliminate a script after 30 pages, but must read the entire script to advance it).

Number of Judges. In this field you can enter the number of judges who must read and rank your script during *this* round of the competition.

Ranking Quantifier. Specify how rankings are quantified for this round (e.g. numerical scores, recommendations, comments, discussions, or a combination thereof).

Cumulative Rank. If advancement is determined by combining the ranks a script receives in *this and previous rounds* enter "YES" in this field. If advancement is determined by the rank/s a script receives in *this round only* enter "NO" in this field.

Of course, this would not apply for the first round (since there are no previous rounds), so for the first round I enter "N/A" (not applicable).

Advancement Threshold. In this field record the threshold a script must meet or exceed in order to advance to the next round of competition. This will typically be one (or a combination) of the following:

1. A set percentage (e.g. top 10% of entries).
2. A set number (e.g. top 25 scripts).
3. A predetermined rank that automatically results in advancement, regardless of the rank received by other scripts (e.g. any script with a score of 60 or higher or any script that receives a recommendation from its judge).

Part C

Part C pertains to the numbers and percentages of scripts judged and advanced relative to the applicable round of competition.

Total Entries. Record the total number of scripts entered into the competition for that competition year. Be aware that you won't be able to complete this portion of the template until the competition closes for entries and releases entry and advancement numbers.

If you're still deciding whether or not you want to enter a competition, you can get an idea of the number of entries your script might go up against by researching the competition's advancement announcements from previous years, since those sometimes include entry numbers.

Judged this Round. Record the total number and/or percentage of scripts judged during this round of competition. For the first round, it should be all entries. For later rounds it will be the number and/or percent of entries that advanced from the previous round.

Number that Advance. In this field enter the number of scripts that advance to the next round.

When a competition advances a predetermined number of scripts (e.g. top scoring 100 scripts), you'll be able to complete this field prior to the competition releasing results. Otherwise, you won't have access to these numbers until the competition starts releasing results and/or advancement information.

Percent that Advance. In this field enter the percent *of total entries* that advance to the next round.

As with the previous field, when a competition advances a predetermined percentage of scripts (e.g. top scoring 25% of entries) you'll be able to complete this field prior to the competition releasing results. Otherwise, you won't have access to this percentage until the competition makes advancement announcements/releases results.

Part D

If you entered a competition that uses format, genre and/or category-specific judging then you will replicate the fields that make up Part D for *each* format, genre and/or category under which you submitted your script/s.

Genre Entered. In this field, record the genre (or format or category) under which you entered your script.

Total Genre Entries. In this field record the total number of entries *for this genre* (or format or category).

Since a competition might allow entrants to enter the same script into multiple genres or categories, the *total number of entries* for a competition might differ from the cumulative number of entries *per genre/category*.

For example, Script ABC might be entered only in the drama category, whereas Script XYZ might be entered in drama as well as sci-fi and also thriller. The *total scripts entered* would be two, but if you added up all the *genre entries* you'd have four entries.

Judged this Round. In this field, enter the number and/or percent of scripts *in this genre* (or format or category) that are judged during this round of competition. For the first round, it should be all scripts entered in that genre/format/category.

Number that Advance. Enter the number of scripts *in this genre* (or format or category) that advance to the next round.

Percent that Advance. Enter the percent of scripts *in this genre* (or format or category) that advance to the next round.

Some competitions aren't always clear if the advancing percentage is drawn from the *total* entries or the total entries *per* genre/format/category. If you want to know for sure, you can always take the *number* of scripts that advance in a genre/format/category and divide that number by the total entries for that genre/format/category.

For example, if a competition receives 600 sci-fi entries and 172 advanced to the quarterfinals, then:

$$172 \div 600 = .2866$$

So, about 29% of sci-fi scripts advanced to the quarterfinals.

Part E

The fields in Part E are used to record the *results* of your entry.

If you enter more than one script, simply replicate the fields in Part E for each script entered (and/or each *version*, if you've entered more than one version of the same script).

Script Entered. Use this field to record the title of the script you enter. I suggest you also record the script's version/draft number since you might enter more than one version or draft (either in the same competition year or future competition years).

If you submit an updated version of your script then indicate in which round the newer version began to be judged (I'll discuss this in greater detail in Section VI).

My Results. Once you know if your script advances (or not), you can record that information in this field.

If your script advances through this round, you can enter "advanced." If not, you can enter "did not advance" or "final round reached."

You can make this field as detailed as you like by including other information you receive relative to your results (e.g. the score/s your script received, how many judges advanced or did not advance your script in a specific round, or a summary of any critique you received from the judge/s in that round).

If your script is entered and judged in more than one genre or category then you can replicate this field for each of those genres/categories since the script's results may vary. For example, a script entered in both historical and drama genres might not advance in the drama genre, but might advance to the semifinals in the historical genre.

Section II

Results, Awards, and Prizes

Now that you have a better understanding of the way in which competitions judge, rank and advance scripts, this section will discuss how and when competitions release results, and the awards and prizes you might receive if your script places.

8

Announcing Results

Competitions announce results in a variety of ways and time frames.

You might receive an email, a letter, or a phone call. Or you might have to check the competition's website or social media page to find the results.

Some competitions announce results of all advancement tiers simultaneously. Others announce the results of each advancement tier separately, spread out over the course of several weeks or months.

When a competition does release results there are usually three aspects to that process:

1. The *advancement announcement.*
2. The *notification* of results.
3. The *promotion* of the winning/placing scripts.

In this chapter I'll discuss each of these steps and explain some of the more common announcement scenarios.

The Advancement Announcement

An advancement announcement occurs when the competition *publicly* releases the titles of the scripts that reach an advancement tier.

This information is posted to the competition's website and can be accessed by anyone.

In my experience, advancement announcements always include the titles of the scripts that reached the advancement tier as well as those scripts' corresponding authors. It's also fairly common for the scripts' formats, genres and categories to be indicated.

In addition to this, when publicly announcing winning or high-placing scripts, the competition might also release those scripts' loglines or summaries. And, on occasion, a competition will provide a small biography of (or letter from) the winning/placing writers.

Some advancement announcements will state the total number of entries the competition received that year and the percent of those entries that advanced.

Finally, some competitions make advancement announcements at events (e.g. festivals, conferences, luncheons, ceremonies). Typically, this is reserved for announcing the competition winner/s. But the corresponding announcement is usually still posted online. Just know that the results might not be posted until hours or days after the announcement at the event.

The Notification of Results

In addition to the public advancement announcement, most competitions will post the announcement (or a notification of the announcement) on their social media pages and send an alert to their email subscribers and/or entrants. Usually these notifications are brief, only indicating that the results have been posted. However, sometimes (especially for higher tiers of competition) the notification may include more detailed information, restating the information included in the advancement announcement—or even including more information than what's contained in the advancement announcement. For example, a competition might only include the titles and author names of advancing scripts on their website. However, in the notification email sent to entrants, the competition might include the number of entries received and the percentage of those entries the advancement represents. Or, especially for higher advancement tiers, notification emails might include biographies of the advancing writers, or the loglines of those advancing scripts.

Notifications can be public (e.g. a social media post) or just to entrants. The content and individuality of entrant notifications vary from a generic email informing entrants that the results have posted online, to personalized notifications informing each entrant of his/her script's results (e.g. placement, scores, highest round reached). Usually these notifications are made in one or more of the following ways:

- ***Email***. Most competitions email entrants when results are announced. Again, these emails vary in detail and personalization. Typically the emails come directly from the competition, but if you submitted to the competition using a third-party (e.g. FilmFreeway or Coverfly), then the notification email might come from that third-party source instead of (or in addition to) the competition itself. Also, if you've purchased or requested written critiques in conjunction with your competition entry, then those critiques are sometimes sent to you separate from notification emails—*but not always*. So if you purchased/requested critiques, it's a good idea to check notification emails to see if your critique is included with that email, or if the email includes instructions on how to access your critique.

- ***Mail***. It's rare, but some competitions do mail paper notifications. These letters may arrive after the online announcements have been made.
- ***Phone Call***. Sometimes, just maybe, you'll get a phone call. Usually a phone call means your script placed highly in the competition, and it typically occurs before the results are publicly announced online. So, if you receive a call from someone at the competition around announcement time, be prepared for some good news.

Combination Delays

It's not uncommon for a competition to use more than one method of notification, but those notifications won't always happen simultaneously or at the same time as the actual announcement. I've seen announcements post to a competition's website weeks before they post the notification to their social media pages. And I've received email notifications that arrive several days after the competition has posted results online. Given this, I add announcement dates to my calendar so I know what date I should check the competition's website for results.

No Notifications

Some competitions don't post or send any announcement notifications. In these cases, you must take it upon yourself to check the competition's website for the advancement announcement. This is another reason I add the announcement date to my calendar—so I can check the competition's website for results, even if I don't receive a direct notification.

Code of Silence

When you've been notified directly about your script's placement in the competition, the competition may require you to refrain from publicly announcing your results. This is because some competitions want to contact all winning/placing writers *before* they make the public announcement. And this notification process takes time.

When I was a semifinalist at AFF, I received a very nice phone call. I was informed of my placement, but asked to keep it quiet until the official, public announcement had been made. Being notified early was especially helpful in this situation because the AFF competition is associated with their conference and festival. Placing in the competition provided me the opportunity to attend specialized seminars and panels at that conference. Knowing early that I was a semifinalist gave me the time to determine whether I could attend the conference and (if so) make plans regarding flights, lodging, time off work, etc. Had I not been able to do this until the public announcement posted I would have had less time between learning about my script's placement and the actual festival, which would have made it far more difficult to figure out the logistics of travel and lodging, time off work, etc. (and the associated trip costs would have been higher).

Promotion

Many competitions promote the writers and scripts that advance to some (or all) advancement tiers. The degree to which scripts/writers are promoted varies from competition to competition, and also from tier to tier. This promotion could range from the competition organizers actively pitching you and your script to industry professionals, to making your script's logline and your contact information available to interested parties (e.g. agents, managers, producers, and/or even festival attendees).

Whatever the case, this type of promotion will likely include:

- Your name and contact information (so an interested party can contact you directly).
- Your script's title, logline/summary, genre, and format.
- Possibly a short biography about you and/or a letter from you regarding your writing experience or writing goals.

It's important to know that some competitions will forward the winning/placing *scripts* to interested parties. If this is the case, be sure you are okay with it and determine if you have any say over who sees your script—and/or if you'll be informed regarding who has requested/received your script.

Personally, I want to maintain control over who sees my script. So, while I'm comfortable with a competition *pitching* my script to interested parties, I prefer that interested parties contact me (the writer) directly if they want to see my script in full.

Including Information

Of course, in order to disseminate the information used to promote you and/or your script, the competition must first gather that information.

If you reach an advancement tier that will result in promotion of you and your script (or, if you reach the tier just before that), many competitions will offer you the opportunity to send them information about your script and yourself (e.g. logline, biography, contact information) so your information can be presented *as you want it to appear* in those announcements/promotions. However, this isn't always the case. So be sure that the information you include on the competition's **entry form** is exactly how you want it referenced on announcements and during promotion.

That said, if you want to use a non de plume, you'll have to check the competition's requirements to see if it is allowed.

Announcement Dates

The time period between when a competition opens for submissions and when winners are announced can be anywhere from a few months to almost a year.

Typically, as soon as the competition opens for entries, they state the dates they intend to announce results. Some targeted announcement dates are very specific (e.g. finalists will be announced on January 15th by 12:00 p.m. PST) and others are more general (e.g. finalists will be announced around the middle of January).

While certain competitions always release results on their targeted dates, other competitions tend to release results a few days (or a few weeks) earlier or later than projected. When this happens, some competitions send notifications to entrants to inform them the projected announcement date has changed, but some competitions don't (perhaps changing the announcement date on their website, but not alerting entrants directly).

I suggest you maintain a record of the various announcement dates for the competition/s you enter. Hopefully, this will keep you from wasting time checking your email or the competition's website for announcements that aren't scheduled to release for another two months. (I speak from experience here. I used to check my email every half hour when an announcement date was looming.) Now I add announcement dates to my smartphone calendar, my wall calendar, and my Submission Template (discussed in Section VII). Once I've done that, I can clear my head-space for something more productive—like working on my next script!

The Waiting Game

It can be incredibly difficult to put a ton of effort into a script, submit it, and then turn your brain off to it.

If you're like me, you fill out the entry form, hit submit, and then want the results the very next day! But, of course, that's not how it works.

Waiting for results isn't easy. And the closer it gets to an announcement date, the harder it is not to hit "refresh" on the competition's web page every thirty seconds, eagerly waiting for those results to post.

So, the advice I give myself (and I hope it will be helpful to you) is: Keep writing.

Of course, once you've submitted your script you might want (or need!) to give yourself a break from writing (a few days or a few weeks)—but after that writing hiatus, my suggestion is to *delve into your next script*.

I'll be honest: it can be jarring going from a polished script to... well, anything else. But I find that working on a different script keeps me from getting fixated on that *one* script and the competition/s I entered it in.

Plus, when the results are finally announced, I have another script already in the works. So, if I do well in the competition, I have another script started that I can mention when an agent, or manager, or producer asks, "What else have you been working on?"

If my script does *not* do well in the competition, then it's a little easier to accept those results knowing that I'm already invested in a new script.

Of course, instead of starting a new script after you hit that submit button, you could delve into rewrites of the script you just submitted. But I've found it's more productive to wait for results and critiques before I do that. But that's me, and you'll figure out what works best for you and your writing process.

Finding out how to be patient, how to set one project aside and start on another, how to stay focused on writing... these are some of the benefits competitions present that are entirely in your control. Entering competitions, waiting for results, dealing with results... all have the potential to help you figure out what works best for you and how the writer in you works best.

9

Awards and Prizes

While a few competitions award multiple winners per competition year (Nicholl, for example, awards up to five fellowship winners per competition year), typically competitions award only one winner. And some competitions award prizes *only* to winners.

However, it's common for competitions to have other **award levels** (a placement in a competition that's accompanied by one or more prizes). And while the prizes that come with these placements aren't as substantial as those that accompany a win, these prizes can still be beneficial. For example, if you place as a Second Rounder at AFF you can attend panels at their conference that are exclusive for Second Rounders and above.

The types of prizes presented by competitions are many and varied. Moreover, the advancement tier your script must reach in order to receive a prize varies from one competition to the next. For example, while some competitions only promote their winning writers, the Scriptapalooza International Screenplay Competition actively promotes their feature winners, finalists *and* semifinalists.

Finally, before I delve into the types of prizes offered by competitions, remember that a competition might alter its awards and prizes from year to year. So always check a competition's current information before entering.

Format, Genre and Category-Specific Awards

Competitions that use format, genre and/or category-specific judging will award a winner (and sometimes other award levels) for each format/genre/category.

For example, to enter a feature script at AFF you must enter the script under either the drama or comedy genre. After that, you can choose to *also* enter that script in one or more of the other genre options (e.g. sci-fi or horror). AFF awards winners (and finalists, semifinalists, and Second Rounders) per genre. However, since every script must be entered in drama or comedy, the cash *prize* for winning in those genres is larger—$5,000 each (versus $2,500 for each of the other genre winners). I should note that AFF awards other prizes also, many of which are associated with their festival and conference.

While some competitions award one winner per format/genre/category, other competitions do the same but *also* award one *overall* or *grand-prize* winner.

For example, PAGE runs one competition per year in which they award gold prize winners in seven feature genres, two TV genres (comedy and drama) and one short category. PAGE *also* awards one grand prize winner that is selected *from the finalists in any format, genre or category*. This means that the grand prize winner is chosen *in addition* to the gold prize winners *and* this means that any finalist script, regardless of format/genre/category, can become a grand prize winner.

Some competitions have a similar award structure, but keep formats separated. For example, Scriptapalooza International Screenplay Competition awards one winner for shorts and one winner *per genre* for features. They also select a grand prize winner, but this winner is only selected from the *feature* scripts. So even though features and shorts are entered in the same competition, they are awarded as if they were separate competitions. Similarly, Big Break® awards one grand prize winner for feature scripts *and* one grand prize winner for teleplays.

It's important to know how competitions define their winners so you can accurately report your placement in any queries or pitches. Also, how competitions define their winners greatly affects the types of prizes the winners receive. For example, the PAGE grand prize winner receives $25,000, while their format/genre/category gold prize winners receive $1,000 each.

Of course, this goes for other types of prizes as well (e.g. script promotion, specialized classes, the amount of mentorship received).

Types of Prizes

Prizes awarded by competitions can range from cash to mentorship, festival tickets to guaranteed representation. What follows is a look at some common types of prizes that often accompany winning or placing in competitions.

Money. Some competitions only award prize money to the winners of the competition. Other competitions also award prize money to those who place highly in the competition (though usually the amount awarded is quite a bit less than the grand prize winner). For example:

- PAGE awards $25,000 to their grand prize winner, $1000 to each genre gold winner, $500 to each genre silver winner, and $250 to each genre bronze winner.

- AFF awards $5,000 to the winner of the drama genre, $5,000 to the comedy genre winner, $1,000 to the short screenplay winner, and $2,500 to each of their other feature genre winners.

- Nicholl awards $35,000 to each of their fellowship recipients. Those winnings are paid out over the course of one year and are dependent on the writer's adherence to the terms of the fellowship.

Hoping to win a cash prize is probably not the best reason to enter a screenplay competition. But, if you *do* win, it can certainly be a nice bonus.

Gift Certificates. Gift certificates aren't a common prize, but they do exist. The dollar value of gift certificates varies, as does the store associated with the certificate (e.g. Amazon.com, iTunes Store, or Starbucks®).

Listings. Prizes could include a listing of your awarded script, your script's logline, and/or your personal profile on certain writing resources, (e.g. InkTip® Script Listing or InkTip® Magazine).

Memberships. Some prizes include memberships to online writing communities or writing databases like the International Screenwriters' Association, TVWritersVault™, or STAGE32®. The length of the membership often depends on the competition and the script's placement level.

Books. Books may be given as part of the prize winnings. Usually, the books pertain to screenwriting and/or selling to the film industry.

Subscriptions. Sometimes prizes include subscriptions to writing-related magazines.

Software. Free (or discounted) writing-related software like Final Draft® or WriterDuet Pro are often given as a prize.

Trophies and Certificates. Some competitions award trophies or certificates. These might be electronic (a banner, certificate, etc.) that can be added to your website, blog, or social media site. Or these could be tangible, which might be mailed to you or presented to you in person if award announcements are made at an event.

Pitches and Meetings. Some competitions will arrange meetings or pitches for you. Sometimes it's for one meeting or pitch, sometimes it's for a week of meetings and pitches.

These pitches or meetings are usually with established writers, agents, managers, producers, and/or the competition organizers. The meetings/pitches are typically for the purpose of furthering your screenwriting education, to assist in polishing your awarded script, and/or to introduce you to industry individuals who may be interested in representing you or optioning your script.

These meetings/pitches might be held online, over the phone, or in person. If they are held in person, usually the competition will award some type of stipend to help offset the cost of travel and lodging.

Fellowships/Mentoring. Similar to meetings, but often longer and more interactive, winning (or placing in) certain competitions gives you access to professionals who will help guide your writing and/or career for a period of time. They may review your work, offer edits, set up meetings with writers, agents, managers, or producers, or offer an internship.

The duration of fellowships/mentoring varies significantly—perhaps a week, perhaps a year—as does the degree of involvement the fellowship/mentoring provides.

Fellowships and mentoring might occur at a specific location which could require you to travel or relocate (depending on the length of the fellowship/mentorship) and the related expenses may or may not be offset by the competition. Other fellowship/mentoring opportunities can be conducted long-distance via phone, emails, etc. Sometimes it's a mix of both (e.g. the fellowship consists of a week of in-person mentorship, followed by weekly phone calls for six months).

Before you enter a fellowship or competition that offers mentoring awards, be certain you are able to commit to the time, travel (or, in some cases relocation and internship) required if you win or place. If you can't, you might have to forfeit your win/placement and the corresponding prizes.

Travel and Lodging Expenses. Competitions sometimes help offset your travel and lodging expenses so you can attend awarded fellowships and mentoring, meetings and pitches. Additionally, if you win or place in a competition that is connected to a conference or festival, then it's likely the competition would help offset your travel and lodging expenses so you can attend.

Sometimes this is done in the form of a cash stipend (which may or may not cover all expenses). And sometimes a competition will provide you with actual plane tickets and lodging. However, if you already live near the location of these meetings, conferences, festivals, etc. you might not receive any stipend, lodging, or travel compensation.

Festival or Conference Passes and Tickets. A competition that's associated with a festival or conference might award discounted or complimentary passes/tickets to that year's festival or conference.

Additionally, winning or placing in the competition might provide entrance to special conference classes, meetings, panels, etc., that are only open to those who placed at a certain level in the competition.

If you plan to attend the festival or conference, this can be a real game changer financially, educationally, and hopefully for your career, too. And if you weren't planning to attend, then winning these prizes could be cause to reevaluate.

Finally, your script's placement might be printed on your festival/conference pass, which can be a nice way for attendees who are seeking new writers or scripts to notice that you're an award-winning writer!

Retreats. Wanna getaway? Some competitions award a writer's retreat so you can get away from day-to-day life and focus on your writing and/or spend time with other writers or mentors, depending on the type of getaway offered.

Circulation/Promotion. Winning or placing in a competition can result in industry interest in your script and/or you as a writer.

Not all competitions actively promote winning scripts or writers. However, some of these competitions have earned so much respect from the industry that agents, managers, and producers eagerly await the competition's results and will reach out to the winning/placing writers based on those announcements (either directly, if the competition releases contact information, or by contacting the competition who would then forward the writer's contact information).

Other competitions take a more active role in the promotion or circulation of winning/placing scripts and their writers. For instance, some competitions pitch winning/placing scripts to their list of industry contacts and, if the contact is interested, the competition will either send them the script and/or provide the writer's contact information.

Finally, as already mentioned, some competitions will arrange meetings for winning/placing writers with industry insiders so the writers can personally pitch their scripts to interested parties.

Whatever the competition's degree of involvement in promotion or circulation, make sure you're comfortable with the process and the outcome. If the competition will make your actual *script* available to interested parties, are you okay with that? Will you be informed as to who requested your script? Do you want the competition to pitch for you? Or would you prefer the competition make introductions only, so you can do the pitching yourself?

Commitments and Other Guarantees. Some competitions promise representation if you win (or place). Other competitions promise to produce your script (or a version of it). And other competitions have a first look clause, or option clause. These guarantees may be great for some writers and/or some scripts. However, I would rather maintain full control of my script and writing career until I have a chance to meet the people who might affect what happens to it going forward.

Other commitments can come with winning or placing (or even entering) a competition, too. Nicholl, for example, places certain requirements on their fellowship recipients. If not adhered to, the recipient might forfeit his/her win.

Also, it's important to note that some competitions require winners (or potential winners) to sign and return an affidavit of eligibility and/or liability/publicity release. Failure to do so could result in disqualification from the competition.

Finally, most competitions reserve the right to use your name, likeness, photograph, personal information, information about your script and/or other writings, any subsequent successes, etc., for promotional or other purposes, within or outside the United States, without payment or consideration to you.

Why?

If you're signed by an agent, or your script is produced, or you win a major award, the competition wants to say they discovered you or helped you on the road to success. Doing so gives credibility to the competition (proving they select quality scripts and promote quality writers). This has the potential to help you, too, because the competition is publicly promoting your success. Moreover, your successes might remain on a competition's website for years, which helps keep you and/or your winning/placing script title in the public eye.

Rights and Ownership. If you enter, advance in, or win a competition, does it change the rights/ownership of your submitted material/s? If so, are you okay with that?

Does the competition guarantee representation if you win? What if you don't win? Is there a first right of refusal or first look clause so the competition's affiliates can option your script if they so choose? Do they *have* to? Does the competition guarantee to make a film version of your script? If so, will you have any say over the process?

As I've disclosed earlier, I prefer a competition that clearly states that the entrant retains all rights to his/her work whether he/she wins the competition or not.

Receipt of Prizes

It's good to have an idea of the approximate date you would receive any prizes awarded to you. This could range from the date you expect to receive free software to the week you'd be traveling to Los Angeles for agent and producer meetings.

Keep a record of these dates. If you don't receive your prizes when expected, you can contact the competition in a timely manner. Additionally, you'll want to be *available* to meet any commitments and/or attend any meetings, classes, events, etc. that result from your winning/placing in the competition.

Multiple Writers/Contributors

It's important to note that prizes are typically granted per *script*, not per *writer*. So, if your script has multiple writers (or contributors), whatever prizes and awards it receives will typically need to be divided *among* the writers *by* the writers.

While it may be fairly simple to divide a cash prize two, three, or several ways, dividing other awards and prizes can be difficult. For example, how does a group of writers share a single festival ticket, a class, a mentorship opportunity, or a phone call with an agent?

My suggestion is for all writers/contributors to decide, *prior* to entering the competition, how they will divide any prizes that may be awarded. Prepare an agreement, have all the writers/contributors sign it, and everyone retain a copy. This is not legal advice; it's just my suggestion. Hopefully, this will maintain peace and harmony among the writers and prevent any issues or conflicts once competition results are announced.

Placement Credentials

Winning or placing highly in a competition is something you can consider adding to your query letters and pitches.

However, before doing so, consider how reputable the competition is, at what tier your script placed in the competition, if the win/placement pertained to the script you're currently pitching or another script you wrote, and how long it's been since you won/placed.

Competition Reputation

The more prestigious a competition, the more weight your placement in it carries with the industry. Winning a competition that is not well known can still be a good thing, but it won't grab as much attention as winning (or even placing in) the more established, respected competitions.

Placement Tier

If you place in (but don't win) a competition, then you'll have to do some research to decide if mentioning that placement will help or hurt you. For example, being a Nicholl semifinalist is likely worth mentioning since the semifinalists represent such a small percentage of the scripts entered. However, mentioning your script was a quarterfinalist in a competition where 25% of entries make up the quarterfinalists might not benefit you as it raises the question why your script didn't advance further.

Which Script

Are you pitching the script that won/placed? Or a different script?

If it's a different script, then mentioning a win/placement may or may not be beneficial. If the win/placement was from a well-respected competition and that script won or placed highly, then mentioning that win/placement could be beneficial because it demonstrates that you, as a writer, have skill. However, there's always the possibility that the recipient of the query letter or pitch will question why one of your scripts won/placed, but not the script you're currently pitching.

I would suggest that before you begin pitching/querying you first do some research to determine how the industry currently views this topic.

Time Since Win/Placement

The more recent your win/placement, the better. If too much time has passed, the recipient of your query letter or pitch might question why your script hasn't sold yet (or been optioned, produced, etc.). So before you include any wins/ placements in your queries or pitches, do a little research to determine what the current consensus is regarding the acceptable amount of time between win/placement and inclusion in pitches or query letters.

Bottom line, it's best to be ready to take advantage of a win as soon as it happens. But, if you're not ready to take this step, savor your win anyway.

Section III

Critiques

Knowing how far your script advanced in a competition is definitely information you can use to assess the quality of your writing. However, knowing the details of *why* your script advanced (or not) can help *improve* your writing. Hence, the written critique.

10

Aspects of Critiques

Written critiques can identify the strengths and weaknesses in a script and the writer's skills as a whole. They can provide a glimpse into how marketable a script is, and how appealing the script is likely to be to professionals in the film industry. Critiques can also help determine the genre/s in which your script excels.

However, those aren't the only benefits of critiques. Critiques can help improve, not only your *writing abilities*, but also your *abilities as a writer* because an integral part of a screenwriting career is learning how to deal with critiques.

If screenwriting becomes your career, then critiques are a part of the business. Critiques come from agents, directors, actors, managers, producers, audiences—pretty much from anyone. So it's in the writer's best interest to learn how to receive critiques without crumbling under the weight of the suggestions, to process multiple (sometimes contradictory) critiques and find a thread of consistency, to dissect critiques to make the changes *necessary* (which aren't always the changes *suggested*), and to be gracious, calm, and thoughtful when someone explains why your script isn't perfect.

Critique Terminology

Written critiques come in many forms, and use different nomenclature. However, the most common terms used for written critiques are:

- Feedback
- Notes
- Comments

Terms used among competitions *do not always equate to the same thing*. Feedback is not always written by your script's judge in the competition. Notes could mean a two-paragraph critique or a two-page critique. And comments might be written solely for the writer's benefit, or primarily for judging purposes.

Moreover, competitions usually refer to the person who writes the critique as either a "reader" or a "judge". These are the same terms competitions typically use to identify the individuals who evaluate your script in the competition. This can be problematic, however, because the individual who writes your critique is *not always the same individual who evaluates your script in the competition*.

So, for consistency and to avoid confusion, in *Screenplay Competitions* a written critique refers to any written evaluation of your script, and the term **critic** refers to the individual who writes the critique—whether he/she is your competition judge or not.

Judge Versus Non-Judge

When I first began entering screenwriting competitions I assumed that when I purchased a written critique in conjunction with my competition entry, the critique would be written by my script's judge in the competition.

Sometimes it is. But this is not always the case because many organizations that run competitions *also* offer critique services. Usually, these critique services are not a part of the competition process and can be purchased at any time during the year.

Often a competition will offer one of their organization's critique services to entrants for purchase—typically at a discount—in conjunction with their competition entries. In most of these situations, these critiques will not be written by your competition judge.

I'm not suggesting that a critique written by your script's competition judge is either more or less helpful than a critique written by a critique service (I've received excellent critiques from both). However, I do believe it's important to know if the critique you'll receive will be written by your script's competition judge or not.

Based on my experiences, when your script's critique *will* be written by its judge in the competition, the competition will clearly indicate this on their website. For example, the competition might say: "Purchase detailed feedback from your script's first round judge" or "Included with your entry you'll receive brief notes from at least two of your script's competition judges, more if your script advances in the competition."

However, sometimes it's not obvious. If you need clarification, you can contact the competition. No guarantees you'll get a response, but it's worth a try.

So, why is it important to know if your critique was written by your script's competition judge? After all, a critique is a critique and an opinion is an opinion—whether it comes from your script's judge or not.

However, when the critique is written by your script's competition judge you'll get more insight into *why* your script did (or did not) advance in the competition. Even if the critique is a short "overall" reaction to your script, the judge usually mentions one or two strengths or weaknesses that indicate why the judge ranked your script the way he/she did. Moreover, sometimes critiques written by your competition judges can provide the added bonus of helping you determine where your script ranked in the competition, as discussed in Chapter 6 "Determining Advancement."

If the critique is *not* written by your script's competition judge then you lose this insight, *but* you gain an extra reaction to your script—one from your script's competition judge in the form of your script's placement in the competition, and the other from your critic (who in this case is not your script's judge) in the form of your written critique.

So, while it can be disappointing (and sometimes frustrating) to not receive a written explanation as to *why* your script's competition judge ranked your script the way he/she did, by receiving two reactions you actually have a little more overall information at your disposal when analyzing your script.

For example, perhaps your script advanced in the competition but received low scores on the written critique. From this, you might deduce that while the critic wasn't overly thrilled with your script, your judge must have found enough value to advance it.

Or perhaps the written critique was full of praise, but your script didn't make it past the first round of competition. From this, you might deduce that while the critic liked your script, your judge didn't rank it high enough for it to advance.

Or maybe the critique and script placement are in sync. This could be a good indicator that your script quality is at the level both critic and judge placed it.

Scores

Critiques are sometimes accompanied by scores (often criteria-specific).

If the competition states that the critique *will* come from your script's competition judge, then the scores that accompany your critique will likely be the scores that were used to rank your script in the competition. Otherwise, it's more likely that the scores accompanying your critique were *not* used to rank your script in the competition (since it's less likely the critique was written by your script's competition judge).

Critic Credentials

Most critiques are written anonymously, so it's unlikely you'll learn the name of the individual who wrote your critique. However, most competitions do provide the *credentials* of their critics. (I already covered a good portion of this under "Judge Credentials" earlier, but I think it is worth repeating here since it can affect how you analyze critiques.)

Some competitions list the minimum required credentials for their critics. Other competitions will include your specific critic's credentials with your critique.

Critics' credentials are quite varied, ranging from aspiring screenwriters, to professional script readers, to competition organizers, to film producers.

I'm a firm believer that anyone can have a valid opinion about your story. Movie tickets aren't just purchased by people who work in the film industry. Most folks have a television in their homes (not just the people who work in television). And each of those moviegoers and television viewers will have an opinion about your story—even though they aren't industry professionals. And their opinions are worth considering since, after all, they come from the intended recipients of your work.

However, those who work in the industry should be better equipped to identify your script's individual strengths and weaknesses, to discern *why* something is or isn't working in the script, and to gauge your story's marketability. And since you'll need to work with the industry to get your script produced, receiving critiques from industry insiders can help you determine the likelihood of that happening with your current script.

On the other hand, sometimes you get critiques from fellow writers who haven't yet received an industry paycheck. While these aspiring writers might not have the same industry insight or experience as other critics, getting critiqued by someone fresh to the scene can provide a beneficial perspective. Perhaps these individuals are more willing to see the potential of something new or different, perhaps they are more willing to promote a good story even if it's not considered "marketable." And sometimes they are more empathetic to your journey because they are traveling right alongside you.

Whatever the credentials of your critics, it's important to know that the critiques you receive won't always agree with each other. And, in some cases, they can be completely contradictory. So, if you're trying to decide how much stock you should put into a suggestion, it can help to know the credentials of the person suggesting it.

Also, it's not only about how *much* industry experience the critic has, it's also about the *type* of films (or shows) with which the critic has experience.

For example, let's say I wrote a family-friendly animated comedy and received two critiques: one from a producer and one from a script reader. Now, initially it would seem like I'd want to pay more attention to the critique from the producer. *However*, maybe that producer specializes in graphic horror, whereas the script reader works at one of the top family-animation studios. In this case, even though the producer can have plenty of valid suggestions, I might actually want to pay equal attention to the comments made by the script reader, since he/she is probably more familiar with my script's intended audience.

One final thought, if you're looking for representation or to sell your script, someone who is working in the industry as an agent, manager, or producer will have a better chance to make that happen than a fellow aspiring screenwriter—discussed next.

Critic's Seeking New Material

Some critics are agents, managers, or producers who are *actively seeking new writers or material.* When they are, typically the competition will clearly indicate this fact on their website.

These critics are often seeking a particular style or genre, so scripts are usually assigned to the critics who are most likely to be interested in them. This is why it's important to select the *right* genre/s for your script and have a solid logline/summary because this information could be used to assign your script to a critic.

There's no guarantee, of course, that your script will end up in the right hands, but if it *does* then there's a chance that by entering the competition and/or requesting/purchasing a critique, someone in the industry might read your script and decide they want to pursue working with you.

Length and Quantity of Critiques

A written critique can range from a few lines to several pages. It might be included with your entry fee or cost over one hundred dollars. Your critique might be written by your competition judge, or it might not. Your critique request/purchase might be for one critique only. Or the number of critiques you receive might be determined by how far your script advances in the competition.

Shorter and Many

Shorter critiques (e.g. one paragraph to one page) usually focus on an "overall" evaluation of your script, possibly touching on a few key strengths or weaknesses. These critiques won't be as detailed or criteria-specific as longer critiques, but they can still be worthwhile.

Shorter critiques are less expensive than longer critiques (usually under $60 or included with your entry fee).

If the critique is very short (e.g. a few paragraphs) it's likely it was written by your script's judge in the competition. This is because some competitions require their judges to write critiques on each script they read *whether the entrant requests the critique or not*. Because of this, the critiques are written primarily for purposes of the competition, not necessarily (or not only) for the benefit of the writer.

Often judges use these critiques to help them rank scripts. Additionally, competition organizers can use these critiques to make sure the rank assigned to a script is consistent with its corresponding critique and the competition's judging criteria. And sometimes these critiques will play a role in determining which scripts advance in the competition (for example, some competitions require their final round judges to take previous judges' critiques into consideration when determining which scripts should win the competition).

Even if critiques are written first and foremost for the purpose of the competition, some competitions will make those critiques available to entrants (as part of your entry fee or at an additional fee). When this happens, the competition should guarantee that you will receive at least one critique, since every script must be judged (and consequently critiqued) at least once. Then, if your script advances in the competition, you might (depending on the competition's terms) receive critiques from some (or all) of your script's judges in subsequent rounds.

Though these types of critiques are usually shorter and less detailed than longer critiques, the potential to receive *multiple* critiques can be very appealing since receiving more than one individual's reaction to your script can be incredibly beneficial.

However, because these critiques aren't very detailed, they won't always give you much guidance or insight into *how* to fix an issue with your script.

For example, a short critique might state that your characters aren't well developed. And that might be the only guidance you get. So, if you think you know how to improve your characters, then these critiques could be sufficient. But, if you need more guidance, then this brief reaction likely won't be enough to really help you.

Additionally, when critiques are written for purposes of the competition, the judges are often jotting down their raw reactions to your script. Therefore, their comments might seem harsh and can be fairly tough to read.

However, just because a critique is penned with the writer in mind, it does not automatically mean the critique will be kindly written. But the chance is greater that the critiques written for competition purposes will be blunt.

Finally, I should note that critiques *can* be written for both competition purposes *and* to help aid the writer. For example, as a Reader at AFF, I was required to write critiques for every script I read whether those critiques were requested by entrants or not. However, AFF Readers were still instructed to write constructive, kind critiques since there was a strong chance the entrant would request our comments. As a Reader, I appreciated this procedure because even if I didn't advance a script, I hoped my comments would help the writer improve his or her script. And, as a writer myself, I appreciate this procedure because it means I will receive something constructive for my competition entry fee, whether my script advances or not.

Longer and Fewer

Longer critiques (about two pages or more) are usually written *because the writer requested/purchased them*. These critiques are written *in addition* to the judging process. Therefore, there's a good chance this type of critique will be written by a source other than your script's competition judge. However, if the critique *is* written by your script's competition judge, then odds are it will be written by your script's *first round judge only*, regardless of how far your script advances in the competition.

Since longer critiques are an added service, and usually a time-intensive one, they typically have a higher fee than shorter critiques, usually starting around $90.

Longer critiques can provide helpful insights since they delve into the details of the script (what works and what doesn't). And it is more likely that these critiques will offer suggestions on how to improve a script.

Don't assume, however, that because these critiques are written with you in mind that they will all be kind and supportive. Some competitions *do* encourage their critics to be kind and supportive, constructive but encouraging—but, even then, it still depends on the individual writing the critique.

Critiques that are about three or more pages generally offer criteria-specific evaluations of your script. Typically the criteria covered is the same criteria used to judge the competition—but, if the critique isn't written by your competition judge, then this might not always be the case. Nonetheless, most competitions will state online the criteria the critique will cover.

Many times a criteria-specific critique will also include criteria-specific *scores*. If the person writing the critique was your script's competition judge, then it is likely these were the same scores used to rank your script in the competition.

Criteria-specific scores can help pinpoint where your writing excels and where your writing needs work. For example, a critic might offer suggestions to improve your script's plot and character. But if your characters scored an 8 out of 10, and your plot scored a 5 out of 10, those scores give you a better idea of where your script needs the *most* work.

With longer critiques you're apt to receive a logline or summary of your script as well as the credentials of your critic. And sometimes it's required that your script's critic state whether he/she would give your script a *Pass*, a *Consider*, or a *Recommend* if the script were to be presented to his/her production company, agency, etc. Sometimes this is theoretical (not all critics currently work in the industry), but sometimes critics *are* actively seeking new writers or material. Because of this, it's important to remember that receiving a Pass, Consider, or a Recommend is not always a reflection of the quality of your script since a critic might Pass on your script, not because it's a terrible script, but because his/her company isn't looking for the genre or style of your script. Typically, however, the critic will explain *why* he/she gave your script a Pass, Consider, or Recommend, which can be quite helpful.

Now, sometimes, a critic will give your *script* a Pass, but give you, the *writer*, a Recommend or Consider. This might be disheartening at first because your critic did not Recommend your script. But since so many screenwriters write on assignment, being Recommended *as a writer* can be a very good thing. Similarly, I've seen comments where the critic would Pass on a script because they didn't feel it was marketable, but suggest the script be used as a "calling card" to market the writer because the script is a strong example of the writer's abilities.

Receiving a Recommend (either for yourself and/or your script) could be worthy of inclusion in your pitches or query letters. But I suggest you conduct research on how the industry views this inclusion when it comes time for you to pitch or write your query letters. Who gave you and/or your script that Recommend? For which organization/company/competition does he/she work? How long ago was the Recommendation given? These are all things to take into consideration to help you decide if including the accolade in your pitch or query letter would be beneficial or not.

Conclusion

So, which is better: one long critique or multiple shorter critiques? It depends on you, your script, and the time and money you have available.

To determine what type of critique might benefit you the most, ask yourself what kind of insight you need. Are you looking for an overall evaluation of your script? Do you want to know how your script ranks relative to specific criteria? If a critic says your dialogue is boring, will you need ideas on how to fix this, or is the comment alone helpful enough? If you are told your script's pacing is off, will you know what to do?

Whatever your answers, I strongly recommend that you *always get more than one critique*—because while one critique can be very helpful, it can also be very misleading (which I'll discuss shortly). If you can't afford two critiques, then think about using your script's rank in the competition as another gauge regarding the quality of your script (but this only works if your judge and critic are different individuals).

Request/Purchase of Critiques

None of the competitions I have encountered *require* you to *purchase* a critique in order to enter the competition.

That said, if you're going to purchase/request a critique, usually competitions require you to make that purchase or request *at the time you enter the competition*. Because of this, I suggest conducting your research about a competition's critiques *before* you start the submission process.

A few competitions do allow you to request/purchase your critique either at the time of entry or some time after entry (up until a specified future date). For example, Nicholl allows you to purchase Reader Comments at the time you enter the competition *or* any time after you enter the competition *up to* December 31st of the competition year. In cases like this, if you don't request/purchase the critique at the time you enter a competition, I suggest you make note of the final opportunity to do so in case you decide later that you do want the critique.

Critique Fees

As mentioned earlier, while some critiques are included in the competition entry fee, others cost an additional fee. Critiques purchased in conjunction with your competition entry typically fall between $40 and $100 depending on their length and whether they are written for purposes of the competition or because you purchased them. It is worth noting that non-competition critique services can be more expensive, and depending on the content and length of the critique, can actually cost several hundred dollars.

Unlike entry fees (which I'll discuss more in Section VI), usually critique fees are the same price *during the entire entry period*. On rare occasions, some competitions do charge more for critiques that are purchased closer to the competition's final entry deadline.

Additionally, while some competitions offer discounts on *entry fees* when submitting more than one script at a time (or one script in multiple genres/categories), I've not yet encountered a "multiple critique" discount. However, I have seen *other* types of critique-related discounts.

Critique Discounts

Sometimes competitions offer critique discounts, coupons, or even free critiques.

These discounts are usually offered around the time the competition opens for entries (to encourage writers to enter early). But I've also seen promotions during events like Black Friday, Cyber Monday, etc.

Often these discounts are announced via email, on the competition's website, and/or on their social media pages.

Multiple Entries

If you choose to enter your script in multiple genres or categories within the same competition, and if you want a critique for each of those entries, you might need to purchase/request critiques *per* genre/category.

For example, as I write this, PAGE allows you to enter your feature script in up to three genres (or the same genre up to three times). You can purchase Judge's Feedback from one, two, three (or none) of these first round judges (but you'll be required to pay the full critique fee for each).

However, just because you've entered your script into multiple genres or categories within a competition does not always mean that your script will be read by multiple judges, which is one reason why you might not be able to purchase/request multiple critiques.

Receipt of Critiques

When and how does the competition actually send your critique to you?

Method

It's been my experience that competitions make critiques available to entrants in one of two ways:

1. Email. Usually competitions will email critiques in the form of a PDF attachment, though some will put the critique in the body of the email.

2. Accounts. Competitions that require you to create an account through their website or a third party in order to enter their competition might post your critique/s to your account (instead of emailing the critique to you). This means you will need to sign into your account to access your critique/s once they are made available. In these cases, often your critiques will only be available for a short period of time. So access your critique/s as soon as possible, then download, print, and/or save the critique/s to safeguard them in your own records.

Date

Critiques become available to entrants in one of three timelines:

1. A few weeks to a few months *after entry*. Some competitions provide a pretty quick turnaround for entry-related critiques. This can be especially helpful if you're trying to make revisions to your script prior to submitting it to another competition.

2. After a script is *eliminated* from the competition and the corresponding advancement announcement has been made. If, for example, your script makes the semifinals, but not the finals, then you would receive your critique *after* finalists were announced. If the competition is emailing critiques, it can take several weeks to get all those critiques sent. You might get your critique the day after the advancement announcement or a month later.

3. After the competition *ends*. Usually this happens when critiques are written by the judges for competition purposes. However, don't expect your critique the day after the winners are announced. It's typical for these critiques not to be released until a few months later.

As stated earlier, when you purchase one of the competition organization's critique services in conjunction with your competition entry, often the competition gives you a slight discount on that critique service. However, be aware that the turnaround time for that critique might be longer than it would have been had you purchased the critique separately from your competition entry.

Timeline Considerations

If you want the option of receiving written critiques to aid you in rewriting your script prior to submitting it to competitions, then you have three basic options:

1. Purchase one or more critique services, receive the critiques, make any necessary rewrites, and then enter the revised script in competitions.

2. Purchase/request critiques in conjunction with your entry in one or more competitions, receive those critiques, make any necessary rewrites, and then submit the revised script to *other* competitions that are still accepting entries.

3. Enter competitions that send critiques shortly after you enter the competition and that allow **resubmissions** and/or allow entries of multiple versions of a script in a single competition year. With this option, you could enter the competitions with the current version of your script, receive your critique/s, make the necessary rewrites, and submit the revised version of your script as a new entry or resubmission (just be aware that very few competitions accept resubmissions and/or allow entries of multiple versions of a script in the same competition year).

The simplest option is the first one. *Usually* the turn-around time for critique services is a few days to a few weeks, and you can purchase these critiques at any time of the year. Critique services are the most flexible option if you prefer to receive critiques before submitting your script to competitions, but they are often the more expensive option. However, if it means entering an improved version of your script, then even though the critique might cost more, the improved script could make your competition's *entry fee* more worthwhile.

The second option (entering a few competitions, receiving their critiques, making rewrites, then submitting to other competitions) will likely be less expensive than purchasing critique services unrelated to a competition entry, *but* this route requires a lot of planning:

- Money. The money you save on the critique purchased in conjunction with your competition entry (as opposed to a more expensive critique service) might be offset by the increased entry fees of the competitions you waited to enter (if those entry fees increased during that time).
- Time. You must receive the critiques from the first competitions *and have time to make any necessary rewrites* prior to the final entry deadlines of the other competitions you plan to enter.
- Information. Will the critiques received from the initial competitions be detailed enough to determine if changes to your script are warranted? If you receive only one critique, are you willing to make changes based on one critic's analysis?

The final timeline consideration requires submitting a new version of your script *either* as an *new* entry or a *resubmission*.

Not all competitions accept multiple versions of a script and/or resubmissions. These options only work if the competition accepts them and if the competition is still open for entries and/or resubmissions when your revised script is completed.

Both resubmissions and submitting multiple versions of the same script are discussed in greater detail in Section VI.

Keeping Records

I suggest you save copies of your critiques in one (or all) of the following folders (all of which can be physical and/or digital):

1. A folder in which you *file all your critiques in one location* regardless of the scripts they apply to or the competition/critique service they came from. This way, you have all the critiques you've ever received in *one* location.

2. A folder in which you *file critiques by script*. I also suggest adding subfolders so you can file critiques relative to each *version* of a script.

3. A folder in which you *file all critiques associated with a specific competition*. This allows you to look back and identify which competitions provided the most helpful critiques.

A Sampling of Competitions and the Critiques They Offer

Here are ten competitions and the type of critique they offer *in conjunction with a competition entry*. Although current at the time I write this, be sure to research the competitions that interest you to determine if this information still applies.

- **AFF**. Brief notes written by your script's competition judge/s. One critique guaranteed, more are possible if your script advances. Included with entry fee. Receive: About two months after competition ends. Term Used: Reader's Comments.

- **BlueCat**. About one page written by your script's first round judge. One critique only. Included with entry fee. Receive: Within one month of entry for earlier entries, longer for entries submitted closer to final entry deadline. Term Used: Written Analysis.

- **Big Break®**. No critiques offered in conjunction with competition.
- **PAGE**. About 5-7 pages of detailed, criteria-specific critique. Written by your script's first round judge. Includes script summary, judge's credentials, Pass/Consider/Recommend decision, and the criteria-specific scores the judge assigned to your script. One critique only. $89.00. Receive: Typically within a few weeks of your script's elimination from the competition (or, if your script wins, after the competition ends). Term Used: Judge's Feedback.
- **Nashville Film Festival Screenwriting Competition**. No critiques offered in conjunction with competition.
- **Nicholl**. Brief notes written by your script's competition judges (about two paragraphs each). Two critiques guaranteed, up to six if your script advances. $40. Receive: September. Term Used: Reader Comments.
- **ScreenCraft** *(runs various competitions per year, so check individual competition's critique specifics)*. About one page critique. Not written by your script's competition judge. One critique only. Includes logline/summary and criteria-specific scores, but not the scores assigned to your script in the competition. $69. Receive: Typically 4-6 weeks after entry. Term Used: Feedback.
- **Scriptapalooza** *(Screenplay and Television Writing Competitions–cannot order a critique for short scripts)*. About 4-5 pages of detailed, criteria-specific critique. Not written by your script's

competition judge. Includes logline, synopsis and criteria-specific scores (*not* the scores assigned to your script in the competition). One critique only. Approximately $115.00. Receive: Typically within a few weeks of your script's elimination from the competition (or, if your script wins, after the competition ends). Term Used: Feedback.

- **Script Pipeline** *(Screenwriting Competition)*. About 1-2 pages of fairly detailed critique. Not written by your script's competition judge. One critique only. $95. Receive: Typically 4-6 weeks after entry. Term Used: General Notes.
- **Sun Valley Film Festival High Scribe Screenplay Competition**. No critiques offered in conjunction with competition.

11

Ways to Analyze and Benefit from Critiques

It's not uncommon for people to hear the word "critique" and assume comments will be negative. However, the truth is, critiques don't have to be negative. In fact, a helpful critique can point out what doesn't work in a script as well as what *does* work.

However, even when critiques are kind and constructive, getting heaps of suggestions on ways you should change your beloved script isn't easy.

And even if you take the emotional aspect out of it, objectively determining which critiques to heed and which to ignore can be a challenge.

What follows are methods that help me deal with critiques. I'm hoping some of these will help you, too.

Be Honest With Yourself

A fundamental skill you need as a writer is the ability to be honest with yourself. No critique, including your own, will ever be as effective as it could be if you're not honest with yourself about the quality of your writing. This is a hard thing to learn, but the more you write (and rewrite), and the more you read and analyze other scripts (and films and shows), the more accurately you should be able to assess your own work.

You don't need to know exactly how perfect (or not) every aspect of your script is (I doubt any writer can do that). Rather, when critiques are offered, you need to honestly assess whether taking the suggestions would improve your script.

One question I ask to ensure I'm honestly assessing my script and the critique is: Can I *explain* my decision to follow or ignore the critic's suggestion? In other words, if I'm going to change something in my script—or if I'm going to reject a suggestion—I need to be certain I know *why*. And the reasons for my answers should always support the story and/or the conveyance of the story.

For instance, can I explain why it's pertinent *to the story* to keep or change a plot, a scene, a character, or even a specific word or a piece of dialogue? It should all matter. It should all have a reason for being in the story in the first place. *If* I'm going to change it, I should know why. And if I choose *not* to change it, I should be able to explain why it's necessary to the story that it remain the way it is and why my assessment is more reliable than the critic's.

Another benefit of this process is that it might help me locate the real source of the problem (if there is one). But more on this later.

Finding Your Script's Genre

If you're not sure which genre best suits your script, critiques can help you make that determination, especially for those critiques that offer loglines and/or summaries (as they might help showcase your script's primary genre/s).

Script placement in a competition can help, too. For example, maybe your script consistently places higher in the romance genre than it does in the comedy genre. However, if you want to have a better idea *why* your script does or does not belong in a genre, the written critique is more likely to provide this information.

Finally, if your script doesn't meet the necessary aspects a genre requires, then you can decide if you want to change your story to fit the genre or find the genre that fits your story.

The First Read

Even if you're able to be objective about your own writing, *you will never be able to read your script for the first time*. For this reason alone, I find it crucial to get critiques of my scripts.

I know how my story ends. I know this before I read the first line on the first page. I can't be surprised by a plot twist. I can't be shocked by the inciting incident. And I can't read my story without already knowing how all the pieces come together because...

I know the story. All of it. Even what isn't on the page.

I know characters' backstories, their unspoken motivations, what they are thinking and feeling at any given moment. I already hear their dialogue in my head, which words are emphasized, and which hesitations mean something more than just a pause to take a breath. I know what happened before the story started, I know what happens after it ends, and every plot twist in between. I know it all... And I can't un-know it.

Now, I *can* give myself some space from my script (a few weeks, a few months, *years* if need be), and when I finally reread my script, I have a better understanding of what it's like to read the story for the first time. If I let enough time pass, I might even forget certain *aspects* of the story (a line of dialogue, a secondary plot point, a vivid image, a clever transition), and this can shed new light on what reads well and what doesn't. Maybe I find myself tripping over some of the dialogue, or find certain descriptions confusing, or realize a couple characters are too similar.

But taking time off from a script is not the same as jumping in without knowing a single thing about the story other than the title.

When someone reads your story for the first time, their critique can help you begin to learn what backstories came through, which ones didn't, what was too confusing, and what was explained too much. You can start to see how others perceive your characters and story *as they are currently written*.

Understandably, when you've put months or years into your beloved script it can be difficult to receive a critique from someone who has read your script only once, and then finds copious flaws and offers a myriad of suggestions on how to make your script better. It hardly seems like they could, or should, be able to offer any valuable insights when you've spent months or years with this story, and they've only spent a few hours.

But remember...

You can never know what it's like to read your script for the first time. So, instead of seeing your critic's lack of familiarity with your script as a negative, look at it as a valid and valuable asset.

Your script can only make one first impression, not just with your reader, but with judges, agents, managers, producers, directors, actors, and *eventually* your viewing audience. So while it might be frustrating to take suggestions from someone after they've only read your script once, knowing how they perceived your script after one read can be crucial.

The Best Version of Your Story

I think it's pretty safe to say that rarely (if ever) does a writer sit down, pen a story from start to finish, and write the perfect script. Perhaps if copious amounts of plotting and planning were done first, then one could come close. But, personally, no matter how much outlining I've done ahead of time, somehow when I sit down and write the *actual* script, issues crop up that I hadn't planned for and that will need to be addressed in rewrites.

Rewrites can range from changing a few words to completely changing the entire script. It's likely the majority of rewrites fall somewhere in between. And that's fine! It's the process. And the process is all about finding *the best version of your story*.

What do I mean by that? I mean that at the heart of your script, you're hoping to make one point—and this is likely your concept or your theme. And there are *so* many ways you can tell a story that center around that concept or theme. However, odds are you have other things you'd like to convey, too: the personality of your protagonist, a secondary theme, a tone. And that's what starts to form *your story*.

That doesn't mean you'll be able to use all these pieces, since every aspect of a story should support the others, especially the main concept and theme. So when all aspects of your story intertwine and support each other, odds are you're getting closer to finding *the best version of your story*.

Sometimes it takes a few months to find the best version of a story, and sometimes it takes years. Sometimes (and don't panic) it can take decades. I choose to believe that the best version of my story is out there—it just depends on how hard I'm willing to work to find it. To create it.

So, when it comes to rewriting, I have to remind myself that as good as a moment might be, if it unnecessarily confuses the audience, if it messes with the pacing, if it undermines a more important point, or if there's another way to write the moment that would carry more impact—then the current moment probably has to go. This applies to lines of dialogue, scenes, characters, secondary plot points, maybe even the main plot—pretty much everything. So, I ask myself: No matter how much I love this moment (scene, character, dialogue, etc.) *is it more important than my story as a whole?* Does this one aspect of my script mean more than what I'm trying to convey with the entire story? If not, then I might have to reevaluate the main point of my story.

It's important to realize that not every single suggestion made by a critic will be right—at least, *not for the story you want to tell.*

It is very possible to receive a critique that is completely legitimate and workable, but is not in line with your vision. The critic isn't wrong, and neither are you. You just have different perspectives regarding your story's direction.

Sometimes it can be difficult to determine which suggestions will steer you towards the best version of *your* story, and which will take you down a path other than the one you'd intended. But the better you understand your story and what you're trying to convey with it, the easier it should be to make these determinations.

Logline or Summary

Summing up your story in just a few words can be difficult. Receiving loglines or summaries as part of your critiques can help you learn how to identify the key aspects of your story, and (depending on how good the critic is at writing loglines/ summaries) give you an idea of how to write a logline/summary in a succinct, intriguing way. Even if you've already written a great logline or summary, sometimes a critic will use a word that's just a bit more accurate or captivating than the one you used—and this can make a world of difference, especially for loglines/summaries where *every word is critical.*

In addition to helping you write your logline/summary, receiving loglines or summaries as part of your critique actually has the potential to offer valuable insights for the *rest* of the critique. Loglines and summaries usually focus on the main plot, characters, and concept of a story, and they can also convey genre and tone. So when a critic writes your script's logline or summary, you have the opportunity to see how he/ she *perceived* your script.

Did the critic's logline/summary include the appropriate main plot, characters, and concept? Or, did the critic perceive the secondary plot, characters or concepts as the main ones? In what genre did the critic classify your script? Was the tone the critic conveyed in the logline/summary consistent with the tone you'd intended for your script?

If the logline/summary accurately encapsulates your story, its tone, and its intent, then there's a better chance the corresponding suggestions will help you achieve the best version of *your* story. However, if the logline/summary is not accurate to the story you want to tell, then keep that in mind as you digest the rest of the critique because the critic's suggestions were intended to improve the version of the story the *critic* perceived.

This doesn't mean you need to ignore every suggestion in a critique just because the logline or summary isn't consistent with your vision for your story. For example, if the critic perceives Sara as your main character instead of Zach, then that critic's suggestions were likely made with the intention of making Sara shine (not Zach). So, while you could still utilize some of the suggestions, you might need to tweak them to fit your story (and also analyze why Sara was perceived to be the protagonist instead of Zach).

Of course, just because the critic perceived your story differently than you intended doesn't mean you wrote the script incorrectly. Consequently, the more loglines and summaries you receive from multiple sources, the more you'll be able to determine how well your *script* conveyed your *story*.

The Script, The Story, The Theme

When you receive a critique, you need to determine if the comments pertain to:

1. Your *script* as it's written (the story that's on the page).
2. Your *story* (the vision you have for your story that may or may not be accurately conveyed on the page).
3. Your story's *theme* (the message or moral of your story and/or your perspective and point of view).

For example, perhaps the critic suggests you alter your climax. Is that because the climax doesn't satisfy the set up (story)? Is that because the story is *written* in a way that doesn't accurately convey *which* moment is meant to be the climax (script)? Or is that because the critic *disagrees* with the statement your climax makes (theme)?

As you improve your ability to discern these differences, you'll be better able to interpret critiques and determine which ones will steer you towards the best version of your story.

Critiquing the Theme

As mentioned above, it is possible that a critic will take issue with the message of the story or the author's point of view. While I believe a critic's personal views on the world should not affect how he/she critiques or judges the quality of a script, it does happen.

When this occurs, you'll likely have to sift through that critique to figure out which suggestions will help you achieve the best version of your story versus which comments would *change* your story to fit that critic's point of view.

Sometimes a critic will suggest changes to the theme, not because he/she has a personal issue with your message or point of view, but because the theme could make your script difficult to sell or produce. A message or point of view might not connect with the majority of audiences. This doesn't mean that your message is wrong or that it isn't important. But it might mean that the script won't attract a large enough audience to cover a studio's investment of time, talent and dollars.

Critiquing the Story

Once you receive a critique, the challenge is to determine if the critic accurately perceived your vision of the story. The answer will dictate how you act on their suggestions.

If a critic understands your vision for your story—great! Odds are the majority of his/her suggestions will help you find ways to convey your story in a more impactful way, find ways to convey your vision more accurately on the page, or steer you toward a better version of your story—but one that will still be in line with your vision.

(Again, this is where loglines and summaries can be helpful, since they offer a glance into how the critic perceived your story.)

But what if the critic is sending you in a direction *other* than what you envisioned? Maybe he/she thinks the story would be better served with a darker or lighter tone, or by changing the protagonist's personality, or by changing the ending. You then have to determine if the critic *understood* your vision but thinks going a different route would improve your script, or if the critic *misunderstood* the direction you wanted your story to take (which I'll discuss shortly).

Even if the critic understood the direction you wanted your story to take, there could be other reasons why the critic suggests a new vision. Maybe he/she believes the new vision would be more marketable, would reach a wider audience, or would make your initial concept carry more impact. But it is still your story. It's up to you to determine the vision you want to follow. Only you can decide if you want to change your vision or find another way to improve your script while still adhering to your original vision.

Perhaps you love the critic's new vision and believe it would be an improvement over yours. And that's fine, too. It's your choice because it's your story.

Critiquing the Script

Sometimes a critic ends up suggesting a new vision for your story not because they take issue with your theme or story but because the theme and story are not accurately represented on the page. In other words, *what you've envisioned isn't what's portrayed in your script.*

This means the critic might not realize he/she is suggesting a "new" vision (because the story you *envisioned* didn't make it onto the page). If that's the case, you might have to analyze the critique very carefully to identify the *source* of your script's problems.

For example, if you receive a critique that suggests your protagonist is annoying and needy, and you're reaction is, "That's not true! My protagonist is wonderful, and giving, and selfless," then you have two possibilities to consider: either the critic didn't connect with your character (which is possible), or the character you envisioned is not represented on your page (which is also possible).

Sometimes it's obvious which is which. But sometimes it's not. And this is one reason why multiple critiques can be so helpful—maybe you get five critiques and only one critic thought your protagonist was needy. Or maybe they all did.

If you determine that your character is *not* reflected on the page as you envisioned, then you can go about rewriting that character to more accurately reflect your intent. If you determine that the character *is* accurately represented and that the critic simply didn't connect with the character, that's fine, too. However, I'd still suggest that you try to determine if there's a reason why the character was misconstrued.

In either case, you'll need to carefully analyze every *other* suggestion from that critic because he/she was critiquing your script *under the assumption that you wanted to write a needy character*, so the rest of the critique will be written based on the vision the critic *thought* you were writing.

Bottom line, whether a critic understood your vision or not, at the end of the day only you can decide if you want to change your script. Just be honest with yourself as to *why* you're making the choices you're making.

Source of the Problem

Perhaps your critic makes the statement that scene 17 in your script seemed unimportant to your story and suggests you remove the scene entirely.

It could very well be that scene 17 *is* unnecessary and needs to be deleted. But instead of immediately implementing the critic's suggestion, first try to figure out *why* the critic perceived the scene the way he/she did.

Remember, the critic isn't familiar with your script (they've only read it once), so while it's possible he/she correctly identified a problem with scene 17, it's also possible he/she erroneously thinks the problem *stems* from scene 17.

In other words, it's possible that a problem with scene 17 does exist, *but the fix actually needs to take place at another point in your script*.

For example, maybe scene 17 seemed unnecessary because it wasn't set up properly back in scene 8. Or maybe scene 17 held a clue meant to resurface in scene 95, but scene 95 was overwritten and the reference got lost.

Being able to identify the true source of a problem can save you from unnecessarily rewriting a perfectly good scene instead of addressing the real problem.

Here's another way to look at it: You probably heard of referred pain. You have an injury in one part of the body, but the pain is felt someplace else entirely (e.g. you injured your neck, but the pain is in your shoulder). "Referred pain" can be experienced in writing.

Maybe you get a suggestion about a certain moment in your script that the critic didn't connect with, didn't understand, didn't believe moved the story forward, etc. So, the critic suggests that you change (or remove) that moment. But you can't fathom removing or changing the moment because it is vital to the story, it is perfect the way it is, and if you change it then the rest of the story (or certain vital aspects of it) will change beyond recognition. Provided you're being honest with yourself, does this mean that the critic is wrong?

Perhaps "wrong" isn't the correct word. After all, the critic's perceptions are his/her perceptions. So you have another option to consider: the possibility that you're *both* right.

Perhaps the critic is correct and the moment in question doesn't pay off. But *you're* also correct in recognizing that the moment is crucial to the story and is written correctly. In this situation, the problem probably isn't stemming from that moment, but rather *from a failure to set it up or have it pay off correctly*.

In other words, you have referred pain in your script—scene 17 suffers from an issue with scene 8, or a problem in scene 95.

And this is something that the critic, after one read, might not be able to pinpoint.

However, you know your story inside and out, so it's up to you to do the sleuthing. You'll need to get to the bottom of what doesn't work, why, and where. *Then* you can go about fixing what actually needs fixing. Because there's no point doing surgery on the shoulder when it's the neck that's been injured.

Finding the source of the problem applies to any aspect of your script. It doesn't have to be an entire scene. It could be a moment in a scene, a single line of dialogue, or it could be an entire character, a concept, a plot twist, the tone... Whatever it is, it's in your best interest to figure out where the true problem lies.

The Critic's Job is to Critique

If it feels like a critic is *only* telling you what's "wrong" with your script, then remember: It's the *job* of critics to search out the problems in your script. If they didn't, they wouldn't be helping you very much.

This doesn't mean there isn't room for identifying where a script excels. And, honestly, knowing what *does* work in a script can be just as helpful as knowing what doesn't. But it's a more efficient use of a critique's page count (and your money) for critics to inform you of what needs fixing versus what's fine as written.

Additionally, it's important to know that it's not always the job of the critic to tell you *how* to fix something. The degree to which a critic provides suggestions on how to address issues in your script, instead of just evaluating your script, usually depends on the type of critique you're purchasing/requesting—and it depends on the critic.

Unkind Critiques

There is a difference between a *constructive* critique and an *unkind* critique.

Just because someone points out problems in your script does not mean that he/she needs to be unkind. Critiques can be full of suggestions on ways to improve your script, but be done in a kind way that leaves you feeling empowered to reach the best version of your story. (It is my experience that many competition critiques do skew toward being supportive, even while pointing out the flaws in my script.)

At some point, however, it's likely you'll get a critique that's unnecessarily harsh or just plain rude. Whether these are written by individuals who are bitter, burnt out, or just having an off day, it doesn't change the fact that these critiques can be very hard to swallow.

However, even if someone is rude beyond belief, it does not mean that his/her suggestions are more or less valid.

The first time I received an unkind critique I was tempted to toss the entire critique aside. I didn't want to admit that the critic could possibly have any worthwhile suggestions about my script. Then I realized that if I ignored the entire critique, I might miss something actually useful. Even though the suggestions were made in a snide way, that didn't make them baseless. By ignoring the critique, the only person I was hurting was myself.

It's understandable that when someone unkindly critiques a writer's work, one might react with: "I'll show them! I'll prove them wrong!" But I have made a conscious decision to approach it differently. I tell myself that I am going to succeed, not to spite that person, but *despite* that person. And if that means recognizing a valid suggestion among the snarky comments, then so be it.

Bottom line, try not to take a critic's poor attitude personally. Instead, comb through the critique to determine if any of the suggestions or insights will improve your script. Learning how to do this will not only help you improve your script, it should help you become a more professional writer.

Besides, an unkind critique can help you appreciate all the kind and supportive ones. And who knows, maybe someday you'll need to write a snarky character and you can use that unkind critique for inspiration.

Try to Find Something

It's important to realize that you don't have to take *every* suggestion from *every* critique. However, if you find that you're disregarding *all* your critiques, then it could be because you're too resistant to hearing any criticism about your work. And while wanting to disregard all critiques is understandable, ignoring them *without a valid story reason* ultimately does not help your script or your screenwriting career.

To avoid that trap, in every critique I receive I *try to find at least one suggestion for alteration that I agree with and can act on.*

I make myself do this because it is too easy to disregard everything critics say and to slip into the attitude of, "Well, they just didn't connect with my story," or "They don't know what they are talking about, anyway." And maybe they didn't and they don't! But by challenging myself to find at least one thing to work with, I'm helping to ensure I honestly evaluate the critique and my script. Consider it an attitude self-test.

Be Selective

Just as it can be tempting to *disregard* every suggestion, it can be equally tempting to *implement* every suggestion.

Sometimes you can be so unsure of your story or your writing skills that you waver and waffle and crumble under the plethora of suggestions in each critique. You find yourself rewriting your script in ways you don't really understand, but since the changes were suggested to you by a critic who must know better than you, then "they must be right."

But critics aren't always right. And they aren't always right about *your* script—because it is your script. It is your story. While critics might be spot on with suggestions, those suggestions might be right regarding the vision of the story *they* see, which might not be right for the vision *you* see. And only you can decide which vision is the one you should follow.

Of course, the more critics that make the same suggestion the more likely it is that the suggestion should be addressed, even if not in the way suggested.

But, if you find yourself trying to implement every suggestion from every critique—take a pause. Just as you need to be able to explain why *not* following a suggestion is the right thing for the story, you must *also* be able to explain why a change *is* necessary to the story.

Multiple Critiques

Critiques can be confusing. What one person loves, another hates, whether it's a line of dialogue, a scene, or an entire script. So I offer this suggestion: if you're going to get a critique, *get more than one*.

Can one critique be helpful? Yes! If it's the right one. Get the wrong one, and it can be devastating. Or wildly misleading. One critique has the potential to substantially help or hinder your script. And since you never know which it will be, getting at least two critiques gives a clearer picture of exactly what in your script actually needs work.

The first industry-style critique I ever got was kind, supportive, and positive. It was a great feeling! Then I got another critique from another organization for the same script (and the same draft of that script). That second critique was harsh, unkind, and it seemed as though the critic was annoyed he had to even read my script.

The first critique made me feel as though I could actually be a screenwriter. The second one made me feel as though I was an idiot for trying.

I am so grateful that the second critique didn't come first. I'm even more grateful the second critique wasn't the *only* one I received. If it had been, I would have thought I needed to drastically change my script, or start on a new story entirely—if I'd even had the gumption to keep writing at all. But, thankfully, I had already received a positive response to my script, so the second critique wasn't as devastating as it potentially could have been.

I requested several more critiques for that same script, and the majority of those critiques fell somewhere between the first two (positive, while still including suggestions for improvement). I took all the critiques into consideration (even the unkind one). I made the rewrites I felt were necessary (while still keeping the tone and vision of my story intact). That revised script went on to become a sci-fi semifinalist at both the Austin Film Festival Screenplay Competition and ScreenCraft's Sci-Fi Contest. An even later version of that script went on to be a sci-fi finalist at the Nashville Film Festival Screenwriting Competition.

However, had I only received *one* critique, whether it was overly positive or overly negative, that might not have been the outcome.

So, how many critiques *should* you get? Ask yourself, "How much confidence do I have in my script as it is currently written?"

I used to purchase critiques from every competition I entered that offered competition-related critiques. Now that I'm a more experienced writer, I'm better equipped to judge my writing and I am better able to dissect and implement the critiques I do receive. As a result, I don't always feel the need to purchase copious critiques. However, I *always* get critiques for a new or revised script. And always from *at least* two sources.

Contradictory Critiques

As I said, critiques can be very confusing. What one person loved, another hated. What one person said was a totally pointless scene, another said was their favorite moment. What one reader felt was perfect pacing, another felt was all wrong.

So, what do I do when I get two critiques that make opposite suggestions?

First, I try to figure out which of the two opposing suggestions would more effectively help me achieve the best version of my story. Perhaps both critiques have merit, but maybe one is more in line with my vision than the other.

Next, I try to determine what exactly the critics were picking up on that *caused* their suggestions. Is there something else causing the contradictory reactions (i.e. "referred pain")? Maybe both critics are right, but for the wrong reasons.

And, sometimes, the critiques aren't as opposite as they first seem. For example, maybe one critic loves your character, Lucy, but another said Lucy was unimportant. Maybe both are right. Maybe Lucy is a fantastically written character, but maybe she doesn't actually do anything to help move the plot forward. If so, you could try to figure out if there is a legitimate way to give Lucy more to do without undermining her character or taking away too much from another character.

You Be the Judge

If you can find the criteria the organization will use to critique scripts, ask yourself, "In which of these criteria does my script excel or fall short? If I were the critic reading the script for the first time, what would I say?"

I like this exercise because it helps improve my ability to assess my own work, and it helps me evaluate my script in ways I might not have considered otherwise.

Even if you think you've identified all your script's strengths and weaknesses, a critic will more than likely still offer a fresh perspective and find weaknesses you weren't aware of, and/or help you solve a problem that you identified but couldn't resolve.

Save, Delete, Test

Finding the best version of my story often means having to delete beloved parts from my script. For the sake of the story, I'll have to sacrifice a beautiful scene, a great piece of dialogue, or maybe even an awesome character. It hurts, it's painful, *but if it makes the story better*, then it's necessary.

So, I thank that moment, or line, or character, for playing its part in helping to get my script to its current version—then I delete it.

Well, okay, I actually don't outright delete it. That's still too painful. And potentially wasteful. Instead, if I have to delete something that I truly love, I'll copy and paste that moment into a new document—just the part I'm going to delete. This way, if I ever need it again (either in future drafts of this script or for a future script), I can easily find it.

These moments become my own "Deleted Scenes" and I can look back on them whenever I want. They've been deleted from the script, but they're not totally gone.

What if I'm not sure if removing an element from my story will make it better? Then I save my current draft, make the deletions, and read the revised script. If the story still works, and the flow and pacing are better, I have my answer.

And once again, I remind myself that no scene, line, or moment should ever be more important than the entire script.

Save Everything

At every point in your writing (not just rewriting), *save constantly*, back-up often, and keep easily identifiable drafts.

Many times I remove a moment, a scene, or a piece of dialogue that is well written but no longer fits the story. Then, after several rewrites, I find that moment is needed again. Maybe I removed another scene so I need the previously deleted explanation. Or maybe the pacing changed. Or maybe a secondary character became important again. This doesn't mean I won't need to tweak that moment if I add it back into the script, but being able to pull the moment from a previous draft means I won't have to start from scratch when I already had that moment figured out.

Another reason saving multiple drafts is beneficial is because sometimes (unfortunately) I make rewrites only to realize I actually made things *worse*. If this happens, having the previous draft of my script allows me to go back to that better version without having to remember everything I'd rewritten and "un-change" all those changes.

When I save drafts (or versions) of my scripts, I implement two methods. First, I save my scripts by title followed by the "version" number (the version representing a major rewrite). Then, I add a second number, which represents a smaller revision (maybe a deleted scene or an added speech). This results in multiple files like "version 1.1," "version 1.2," "version 3.7"—but I have *everything* saved.

When I'm going to make a change that I'm not sure will work, I'll indicate the alteration in the script's file name. For example, I might save a draft as "version 4.5 includes dinner scene" and save the revised version as "version 4.6 no dinner scene." With this method I know that the draft before 4.6 has "the dinner scene," so if I decide later that I need to add the dinner scene back into the script, I can locate *the most recent version of that scene*.

Use a system that works for you, whether it's the names you assign your documents, the folders you place them in, or some other technique—it just needs to be clear, consistent, and make sense to you.

Time

Learning the writing (and rewriting) process that works best for you can be a huge help in dealing with everything from plotting your story to implementing critiques and final edits.

For myself, I've found that one of my most effective writing tools is *time*.

Give It Time

As soon as I finish reading a critique, I often feel a frantic need to immediately start working on rewrites so I can implement the suggested alterations. Sometimes this reaction is out of inspiration and sometimes it's out of desperation. Critiques can make you feel excited or terrified. But making decisions about your script (or your writing career as a whole) while on those emotional highs or lows might not always result in the best decisions. I've found that time provides me with better perspective.

Time ensures that I've given the suggested changes enough thought—that I've thoroughly considered how those changes will affect *the entire* story... each character, each plot thread, every moment of pacing. I find it simpler to let this process occur in my own head or on a notepad instead of in a draft of my script because I might discover that the change doesn't actually work as I'd hoped.

That said, for me, it is important to *record* any changes I'm considering. Whatever ideas and rewrites are zooming around my brain, I write them down in as much detail as I can—separate from my script. This way I don't actually change my script until I've had time to fully consider the changes. If the changes still sound good and workable after a day or two, a week, or a few months (depending on the complexity of the changes), then I start the actual rewrites.

For some writers it *might* be necessary to start implementing changes right away. There's nothing wrong with that. My only suggestion would be to save a draft of your script *prior* to making any changes (maybe even include the words "version sent to competitions" in the file name). That way, as previously mentioned, if you make changes and decide in a week's time that they don't work, you can go back to your previous version and start again (instead of having to try and remember every scene or word you changed).

Take Time Off

Taking time off from my script can make it significantly easier to identify which aspects of the script are working and which are not.

When I'm editing and rewriting, I sometimes sit at my computer for eight to ten hours at a time working through the script and thinking of nothing else as I keep all the little details, plot points, threads, arcs, and words at the forefront of my thoughts. Breaking that flow would cause those pieces to fall and scatter and I might have to start all over.

However, once I've gone through that process, I actually *need* all those little pieces and tidbits to fall away so I can see how my edited script reads, without all those cobwebby editing details cluttering up my analysis of the story as it's actually written. The amount of time I need to take away from my script in order to achieve this can vary from a few weeks to several months.

If I'm stuck on something small (a word choice, a phrase, a character's clever comeback) I might not need to step away for days at a time. Honestly, sometimes a two-minute change of scenery has been enough for the solution to present itself.

Other times, when I'm dealing with a major plot point or even the entire script, I might need to step away for several months before I can read the script again and accurately assess it's quality and see a solution.

But again, these are techniques that help me. Everyone's process will be different. What matters is finding the one that works for you.

It's Never Finished

"How do you know when your script is finished?" It's a question I've asked myself often. And I've heard copious writers ask it of professionals time and time again. But rarely do I hear a satisfactory answer.

I think the reason for this is: whatever story you're writing, it's never finished.

Scripts are written, edited, purchased, rewritten, filmed and *still* scenes end up on the cutting room floor. Even after films or episodes are *released*, filmmakers find aspects of their completed projects that, in retrospect, they would change. Even though numerous eyes have seen and approved the final product, there are still aspects that could be improved.

At some point, however, you get to a place where the improvements become increasingly minor, and you have to decide when to keep working on those improvements, and when your time is better spent working on something new. The amount of time it might take to get a script from 98% to 99% "finished" could very easily be the same amount of time it takes to get a new script from 0% to 50%.

This isn't an excuse to *not* polish your script. But at some point you might have to say *it's as finished as it needs to be*. It's the Law of Diminishing Returns.

And sometimes a script is as finished as you can get it *before you need another opinion*. In this case, you might decide to submit your script to competitions or pay for critiques—even though you know your script isn't "finished."

Don't Ignore the Good

Knowing what *does* work in a script is just as important as knowing what does not work. So, while critiques are rarely (if ever) all positive, sometimes they do include a few positive comments—and when you get those, I think it's important to savor them.

A positive comment can help prevent you from rewriting a perfectly good moment in your script. And if you see the same *type* of praise from multiple sources over multiple scripts, then you can get an idea of your strengths as a *writer*. Is your dialogue always complimented? Your pacing? Is your formatting spot-on? Maybe your plots are always really unique. Whatever it is, be grateful for those times when your talent and hard work are recognized.

Keep Writing

When I receive a critique, especially a negative one, the best thing I can do is get back to writing—not the script I just received a critique on, but another script I've already begun.

Don't let one critique get you down. You are more than one critique, and if you want a screenwriting career, then you are more than one script.

Getting back to work is a wonderful reset—at least for me. It reminds me that all my hopes and dreams are not pinned to the script that just got critiqued. And most importantly, it reminds me that I love to write.

Section IV

Eligibility Requirements

To enter a screenwriting competition, each *script* and each *writer* must meet the eligibility requirements specified by the competition, otherwise the entry will be disqualified and any associated entry fees may not be refunded.

Eligibility requirements might be listed under categories, like: terms, terms and conditions, guidelines, requirements, rules, qualifications, agreements, etc.

Some competitions list all their requirements on one web page, and others pepper the requirements across multiple web pages. Sometimes all requirements will be listed before you begin the submission process, while other times requirements aren't mentioned until you have nearly completed the submission process.

In this section I'll discuss some of the requirements you're likely to encounter. However, since each competition has it's own specific requirements this won't be a comprehensive list. You will need to exercise your own due diligence for each competition you enter. Again, it is imperative that you read any and all information pertaining to a competition prior to entering—*each and every time you enter*. I cannot stress how important this is. Eligibility requirements, terms and conditions, rules, guidelines, privacy policies, fine print, etc., can all change with the click of a button, so be sure you read the most up-to-date requirements and understand what you're agreeing to.

12

Script Eligibility Requirements

Each script you submit to a competition must meet that competition's eligibility requirements.

Has the script ever been optioned or sold? Is it 100% your original work? Has it been adapted, either from your own work or someone else's? What is your script's page count? Is it formatted for film, television, a digital series? Is it a short film script? What genre is it? Is it available in PDF format? Did the script already place in this or another competition?

If the entered script fails to meet all eligibility requirements, it (and possibly any other scripts you submitted to the competition) could be disqualified and your entry fees might not be refunded.

What follows are some of the more common *script* eligibility requirements you're likely to encounter.

Accepted Scripts

Not every competition accepts every type of script (format, genre, or category). When you start researching competitions, first make sure the competition accepts the type of script you've written.

Script Format

While many competitions judge feature film scripts, short scripts and teleplays, not every competition judges each format (Nicholl, for example, only accepts feature scripts).

Some competitions judge all accepted formats together, and some organizations run separate competitions for each format (e.g. one competition for feature scripts and another competition for teleplays).

Additionally, determine if the competition accepts spec scripts, shooting scripts, or both (and adjust your script accordingly, if you so choose).

It's worth noting that not all screenwriting competitions accept full scripts. For example, a few competitions only allow you to enter a *portion* of your script (e.g. the first ten or thirty pages). Other competitions are script-*related* but don't judge *actual* scripts (e.g. competitions for loglines, script concepts, reality show concepts, or pitchfests).

Genre

Most competitions accept all genres. Some competitions only accept *specific* genres (e.g. only horror). Others accept most genres but *exclude* specific genres (e.g. accept all genres *except* horror).

Category

Competitions somctimes have judging categories that are targeted to a specific type of story. For example, a competition might have a category for "scripts with strong female protagonists" or "stories set in the Midwest." Or, categories could pertain to the script's writer. For example, "scripts written by authors under the age of 18."

Shorts

It is rare for competitions to use genre or category-specific judging for short scripts. Typically, they will judge all short script entries together.

Teleplays

As stated earlier, if a competition judges teleplays, typically they only accept original television *pilots*. However, some competitions, like AFF, do accept specs for existing series, as well as digital series. In these cases, typically each format will be judged separately (e.g. teleplay pilots and teleplay specs will be judged as two different categories).

If teleplays are judged by genre, usually only two choices are offered: comedy or drama. However, some competitions categorize teleplays by *length* instead of genre: half-hour or hour. And some teleplay competitions *combine* length and genre: half-hour comedy or hour drama.

But... not all comedies are half-hour, and not all dramas last an hour. So, if your script doesn't fit the traditional "half-hour comedy" or "hour drama" it may leave you wondering which category/genre you should enter your script under, or even if you *can* enter. If you're not sure, contact the competition and ask.

Adaptations

Did you base your script on a book? A fairy tale? How about a book *you* wrote and published? Each competition has slightly different requirements regarding adaptations.

The majority of competitions will accept script adaptations of *your own* work (e.g. a script adaptation of your novel, article, poem, etc.) provided none of the material relative to the script was produced for the screen in any way and that you still maintain (and in some cases have *always* maintained) all rights to the work.

If your script is an adaptation of *others'* work/s, then in most cases the script will not be eligible for entry. However, while rare, some competitions do accept adaptations *provided you have the rights to the adaptation and/or the material is in the public domain.*

When submitting scripts based on others' work, you may be required to disclose that the script is an adaptation. The information is usually required at the time of entry (e.g. on the entry form, within the script's logline, on the script's title page, and/or as a supplemental document).

Furthermore, you may be required to provide documentation (either at entry or a later date), proving you have the permission/rights to the adaptation and/or that the story is in the public domain, and that your script does not violate any copyrighted material. This information might be required on the entry form, within the script's logline, on the script's title page (or as the first page of the script), and/or as a supplemental document.

True and Historical Events

Most competitions will accept scripts based on true and/or historical events. However, the competition may stipulate that the script must be based on *more than one* source material.

As with adaptations, some competitions require you to indicate at the time of entry if your script is based on true events. This information might be required on the entry form, within the script's logline, on the script's title page (or as the first page of the script), and/or as a supplemental document.

Also, you may have to send documentation (either at entry or a later date) proving you have the permission/rights to the story and/or that the story is in the public domain and that your script does not violate any copyrighted material.

Page Counts

Some competitions *require* scripts to adhere to a specified page count and will disqualify any entries that fall outside this range.

Feature length scripts usually fall between 90 and 120 pages; shorts fall between 20 and 50 pages; teleplays fall between 22 and 45 pages (if it's a 30-minute show) or 45 and 70 pages (if it's a 60-minute show). However, not all competitions require scripts to conform to these standards.

For example, as I write this, feature scripts submitted to ScreenCraft's Sci-Fi and Fantasy Contest must be no less than 75 pages and no more than 150 pages. Feature scripts submitted to their Comedy Screenplay Contest, however, must be 140 pages or less.

Some competitions allow you to enter scripts that exceed their requested page count, but will charge a fee to do so (either a flat fee or a per page fee). For example, feature scripts submitted to ScreenCraft's Screenwriting Fellowship can be between 75 and 140 pages. However, if a script is between 121 and 140 pages, it will be subject to an additional page overage fee.

Finally, many competitions only *recommend* that your script adhere to standard page counts, but failure to do so may negatively affect how your script is ranked in the competition.

Age of Script

It's rare, but some competitions require you to submit *only* new (or fairly new) scripts.

For example, the 2018 BlueCat Screenplay Competition would not accept scripts that were submitted to any competition prior to February 1st, 2015.

Rights/Ownership/Production

In order to enter a script in a competition the script must be wholly owned and controlled by its author/s. The script can't be currently under option, in production, or in any way tied to a third-party. Even if your script received a first look it may be ineligible.

If your script was sold, optioned, represented, etc. *in the past* but the rights have since *returned to you*, the script may or may not be eligible for entry depending on the competition's eligibility requirements.

Moreover, if the script (or a version of it) has been produced for the screen in any way, then the script will likely be ineligible for entry. For example, if your feature-length *script* has never been produced, but a *short* version of that same script *was* produced, then your feature script might not be eligible.

Lastly, if something happens that changes the rights to your script before the competition ends (e.g. your script is optioned while the competition's judging process is still underway), then it may result in your script's disqualification from the competition. But I'll discuss this in further detail in "Duration of Requirements."

Previous or Concurrent Entries and Wins

What if you want to enter a competition but you entered your script in that same competition in a previous year? What if the script already won the competition? What if you entered the same script in a *different* competition? What if that script won a competition five years ago? Does any of this affect your script's eligibility now? Possibly.

Entries or Wins in Same Competition

Some competitions allow you to submit your script (or different versions of your script) as many times as you choose per competition year. If you're willing to pay the entry fee each time, you can keep submitting (I wouldn't exactly recommend this, but it is possible).

But many competitions do not allow you to submit your script (or even different versions of it) more than once per competition year. And if you try to outsmart the system and enter the same script under a different title then you'll likely be disqualified from the competition (and your entry fees probably won't be returned to you).

However, even if the competition only allows you to enter a script once per competition year, most competitions will *not* limit how many times you can enter the script in their competition year after year after year (either with the same script or an updated version). Of course, this only applies if the script still adheres to all other eligibility requirements.

However, if your script *placed* in the competition previously, then there's a greater chance it (and versions of it) won't be eligible for entry again.

So, *should* you enter the same script in the same competition year after year? To help make that decision, I ask myself the following questions: How far did my script advance the first time? Did I make revisions that I think will significantly improve my script's rank? How did my script rank in other competitions? The answers to all these questions will help me determine if I'm willing to risk my entry fee and try again.

Entries or Wins in Other Competitions

It's rare for a competition to preclude scripts from entry just because they've been *entered* in other competitions (either in the same or previous years). The most common exceptions would be if you entered a competition that included a "first look" type clause, or if entering a competition previously dated your script (see "Age of Script" discussion earlier).

If your script won or placed in another competition it *could* cause your script to be ineligible for entry. Sometimes just the fact your script won another competition is enough to make the script ineligible for entry. But typically it is the prizes associated with a win (or placement) that cause ineligibility as they often affect the script's (or the writer's) *ability to meet (or maintain) the competition's other eligibility requirements*.

For example, the script might be ineligible for entry if it's win/placement changed the rights/ownership of your story or results in the script (or a version of it) being produced for the screen.

It's important to note that, if you win one competition while your script is still in contention at another competition, you might have to inform the second competition of your win. But this will be discussed further in "Duration of Requirements" towards the end of this section.

Finally, winning or placing in competitions has the potential to affect eligibility requirements in other ways too, but these will be discussed in the next chapter as they pertain to the eligibility of the writer, not just the script.

13

Writer Eligibility Requirements

Writers, like their scripts, must meet a competition's eligibility requirements. And, like nearly everything else, writer eligibility requirements vary from competition to competition. So, at the risk of sounding repetitive: always, always, always read all eligibility requirements and fine print from the competition you enter—every time you enter.

That said, what follows is a quick look at some of the more common screenwriting competition eligibility requirements that pertain to the *writer* (or *writers/contributors* if there are more than one per script).

Age of Writer

The majority of competitions require entrants to be 18 years of age or older on the date of entry. However, a few competitions are open to writers under the age of 18. And a few competitions (or categories) are directed at students and/or those under the age of 18.

Location

Most competitions accept international submissions provided the script is written primarily in English.

Entry categories/awards can be location specific (e.g. best screenplay set in the France or best screenplay by an international writer).

Gender

Gender is usually a non-issue, except when competitions offer gender-specific entry categories/awards (e.g. best script by a female writer).

Submitted by the Writer

Entries must be submitted by the script's writer. If the script has more than one writer/contributor, then it must be submitted by all writers/contributors, or by one of those writers/contributors with the permission of all the others.

Earnings

Most competitions specify an earnings limit that, if reached or exceeded by the writer or writing team, would preclude entry. These earnings pertain to the *writer/s* not the *script*. So even if the script you want to enter has never been purchased, optioned, etc., if *you*, the writer, earned money from a screenwriting endeavor, your script could still be ineligible for entry.

The type of earnings that apply toward the limit varies by competition, but usually any earnings from screenwriting endeavors apply (e.g. selling a script or writing for television). And sometimes competition and/or fellowship winnings apply as well.

As I write this, most earnings limits start around $25,000 (though I've seen higher minimums). And some competitions do not specify a dollar amount but state that entrants cannot earn a living writing for the screen.

Finally, if the script you want to enter has more than one writer/contributor then you'll need to determine if the earnings limit applies to each writer *individually* or all writers *collectively*.

Fellowships

Fellowships typically have similar eligibility requirements as non-fellowship competitions. However, it's likely you will be ineligible to enter a fellowship competition if you currently hold a fellowship or if you previously won or held another fellowship (whether with that organization or another organization).

Moreover, each organization has slightly different definitions regarding what *constitutes* a fellowship, so check the requirements for the fellowship you want to enter. If you're still not sure, contact the fellowship for clarification.

Maximum Entries

Some competitions limit the number of scripts you can enter per competition year. For example, Nicholl only allows each writer to submit a maximum of three scripts per competition year.

Previous or Concurrent Entries and Wins

What if a writer entered a competition in the past? What if a writer *won* a competition in the past? What if a writer held a fellowship? Does any of this affect that writer's eligibility now? Probably.

Entries or Wins in Same Competition

Most competitions do not put limitations on how many times a writer can *enter* their competition.

However, it is possible that the competition will preclude a writer from entry if he/she *won* (or *placed* in) the competition in the past.

Typically this is because winning (and sometimes placing) comes with fellowships or prizes that affect a writer's ability to maintain the competition's other eligibility requirements.

Entries or Wins in Other Competitions

It's rare for competitions to preclude a writer from entry just because he/she *entered* other competitions (either in the same or previous years).

Similarly, if a writer won or placed in another competition it *usually* won't preclude the writer from entry—*unless that win/placement affects the writer's ability to meet (or maintain) the competition's other eligibility requirements.* For example, the writer might be ineligible for entry in one competition if his/her win or placement in another competition included a fellowship or a cash prize that exceeds the allowed earnings.

Multiple Writers/Contributors

Entries with more than one writer/contributor can only be submitted if each writer/contributor agrees to enter the competition. Some competitions will require each writer/contributor to send documentation pertaining to their connection to the entered script. This documentation is usually required within a specified time frame after the script is entered.

It's important to note that *each* writer/contributor must meet the competition's eligibility requirements.

Sometimes requirements apply to the writers individually and other times they apply collectively. For example, if the competition has a $25,000 earnings limit, often this applies to the writers collectively. So, if one writer earned $5,000 and another $21,000, the script would be ineligible.

Maximum *entries* typically apply to writers cumulatively as well. So, if Bob and Sue wrote a script together and submitted it to a competition that accepts three entries per writer per year, then that one script would count as one entry for Bob *and* one entry for Sue (meaning Bob could submit two more scripts, and Sue could submit two more scripts).

Some competitions won't accept scripts written by multiple writers/contributors. And, of the competitions that do, some will cap the number of writers/contributors allowed per script, and/or specify the degree of involvement of each writer/contributor with the script. For example, Nicholl will only accept scripts written by one or two writers, and each writer must have *equal* participation in *every* aspect of creating and writing the script.

Verification

If your script places or wins in a competition, some competitions will require you (or all of the script's writers/contributors) to sign and return a verification of eligibility, a release of indemnification, and/or other documents. Failure to return the completed and/or signed documents (or failure to return them within the specified time frame) could cause you to forfeit your win/placement and any prizes/awards that come along with it.

14

Duration of Requirements

Let's say you enter a competition that has a $25,000 screenwriting earnings limit, and at the time of entry you haven't earned that amount. However, at some point during the competition's judging process you sell one of your scripts for $100,000. Are you now disqualified from the competition? What if this sale happens after the judging process has completed but before the final announcements have been made? Or, what if you won a fellowship and you sell your script *during* the fellowship period? The answer: It depends.

Some competitions state that provided you meet the eligibility requirements *at the time you enter the competition* then that's sufficient. If something happens to you or your script *after* you've entered the competition, you can remain in the competition.

However, some competitions state that you and your script's eligibility must remain unchanged *throughout the judging process*. For example, if your script is eligible when entered but is optioned while the judging process is still underway, then your script becomes ineligible. In this case, you would need to inform the competition of the change, and then your submitted script would be removed from the competition and your entry fee may or may not be refunded.

Some competitions state eligibility requirements must be maintained until the competition has officially ended (after they announce the winners and/or after all awards and prizes have been distributed). Again, if your eligibility changes before this deadline passes, you'll have to inform the competition of the change and possibly forfeit your entry fees and any awards and prizes you might have won.

Finally, if you've entered a fellowship, you'll need to determine the eligibility requirements that must be maintained *throughout* the fellowship period. Some fellowships encourage you to make script sales during the fellowship, but this might not always be the case.

Section V

Selecting Competitions

I want to devote this section to a few key considerations to keep in mind as you conduct your own research in order to narrow down your list of potential competitions to enter.

15

Where to Begin

You can learn about the different screenwriting competitions from a variety of sources: books, blogs, podcasts, websites, film festivals, etc.

However, once you've narrowed down your list of competitions you may want to enter, always read the information provided directly by a competition. Don't rely on another person's or organization's interpretation of a competition's process, prizes, fine print, eligibility requirements, etc. You must do this final step yourself.

Top Lists. If you conduct an Internet search for "Top Screenwriting Competitions" you'll get copious results. However, just because someone came up with a "top ten list" doesn't mean those are the top ten screenwriting competitions *for you*.

That said, the more you research, the more you'll see the same competitions appear on lists over and over. This is probably a good indication that the competition has garnered respect in the industry and that winning (or placing) in that competition would be beneficial to your screenwriting career.

Compilation and Review Sites. Several organizations compile lists of screenwriting competitions. These lists may be purely data driven (e.g. listing competitions by approaching deadlines) or they may be more interactive, including reviews and ratings from other writers who entered the competitions in the past.

If a competition receives positive reviews from multiple writers/sources on multiple compilation/review websites, that's a good indication the competition is worth researching. However, databases aren't always comprehensive. And just because a competition *is* or is *not* listed on these sites doesn't mean the competition is or is not reputable. So use multiple compilation/review sites for your research.

Some compilation/review sites allow you to narrow your search by specific attributes (e.g. "competitions that accept feature scripts" or "competitions that provide written critiques").

While many aspects of compilation/review websites are often made accessible to the public without requiring registration, you may be required to register with the compilation/review organization in order to fully access all their resources and databases.

If you register with these organizations and/or sign up for their email list, many will send you periodic emails that feature new or upcoming competitions. This can help introduce you to those new competitions, or make you aware of the competitions you might have missed during your initial research efforts.

Some examples of compilation/review sources are:

- FilmFreeway
- MovieBytes®
- International Screenwriters' Association
- Stage 32®

You can find competition reviews elsewhere, too (e.g. third-party submission organizations like Coverfly, screenwriting-related social media sites, blog comments, etc.).

Just be aware that reviews might not always pertain to the actual *competition*. Social media reviews, for example, might pertain to the competition's social media page (not the competition itself), or compilation/review websites' ratings might pertain to a festival associated with the competition (if applicable), not the competition itself.

Screenwriting Books. Books on screenwriting and/or selling to the film industry may mention screenwriting competitions. If so, it's possible the author will give an opinion on which competitions he/she thinks are worth entering.

Industry Insiders. If you take screenwriting courses, read blogs, listen to podcasts, attend festivals, etc., keep your ears open in case any of the industry insiders mention competitions that they believe are beneficial to writers.

Screenwriting Competitions. Screenwriting competitions occasionally recommend *other* screenwriting competitions. So if you're signed up for a competition's email list, they might alert you to other competitions that you could further research.

Screenwriting Community. You can always look to the writing community and ask fellow screenwriters for their suggestions and opinions.

16

Honing Your List

Whether you are a new screenwriter hoping to discover how your script ranks or a seasoned screenwriter hoping to find representation, how do you go about selecting competitions that are worthy of your script, your entry fee, and your objectives?

First, *identify what you want to gain from the competition process*. Once you've done this, you'll be better equipped to select the competitions that are most likely to meet your objectives. (It's been my experience that the benefits of screenwriting competitions often fall into two main categories—exposure and information—both of which I'll discuss later in this chapter.)

Second, no matter what you hope to get from the competition process, it's a good idea to consider a competition's reputation and the type of scripts it awards.

Reputation

It's important to enter legitimate, well-run competitions, and (especially if you are seeking exposure) those that have garnered respect from the film industry.

If a competition is recommended often, year-after-year, by several reputable sources, then that competition is probably worth including on your list of competitions to research further.

But new competitions come into existence every year, and therefore will not have any reviews. In these situations you need to assess the information the competition provides and determine how comfortable you are entering based on that information (the credentials of the competition organizers, the judges, the competition's judging process, fees, awards and prizes, fine print, etc).

Awarded Scripts

Consider entering competitions that are most likely to award the *type* of script you've written. This goes beyond script format and genre to the *type* and *tone* of stories a competition typically advances. For example, if a competition accepts all genres, do they typically *award* all genres? Do they typically award dramas? Comedies? What about tone? Light? Dark? Mainstream? Edgy? Is there a difference between the type of scripts that make the quarterfinals and those that win?

While this is hard to decipher from a script's title alone, sometimes competitions post the loglines or summaries of the winning/placing scripts (which should give you more insight into the tone of the previously awarded scripts).

Additionally, many competitions include a "Success Stories" section on their website that they update when any of their **alumni** (writers who have placed in or won their competition in the past) garner film-related successes. I find this helpful as it can offer more insight into the type of scripts the competition awards (e.g. If a winning script gets produced you'll likely be able to find more information on that story, it's genre and it's tone. Or, if a winning writer pens an episode of an existing series, you can find out the style and tone of that show).

None of this will yield perfect clarity regarding which competitions you should enter, but it's an effort to gather as much data and information as you can, so you can make the most informed decisions possible.

Seeking Exposure

If you're confident in your writing and confident that your script is ready for the marketplace, then your reason for entering competitions might be to gain exposure. You're ready to start (or progress) your screenwriting career. In other words, you are going for the win—or a high placement—in the hopes it will jumpstart your career.

It is important to identify the kind of screenwriting career help you need so that you can select the competitions most likely to provide that help if you win/place. Do you want mentorship? Guaranteed representation? Do you want the competition organization to arrange meetings for you with agents, managers, and producers? Do you want the competition to circulate your script's logline to industry professionals? Are you hoping the judge who reads your script is so impressed that he/she wants to represent you, whether your script wins or not?

What follows are some topics to consider, depending on the type of exposure you're after.

Reputation and Promotion

Some competitions have garnered such industry respect that they don't have to promote their winners at all—the industry eagerly awaits the competition results so they can contact the winning writers.

But it *is* possible to win a competition and garner little to no industry exposure. Some of the smaller or newer competitions might not have enough notoriety or enough contacts to promote winning scripts or generate much interest from the industry. This doesn't mean these competitions can't offer other benefits (maybe they set up fantastic mentorship opportunities for their winners or offer amazing critiques), but if you're hoping that winning or placing in the competition will set your phone ringing with calls from top film producers, then know that not all competitions excel equally in this area.

Many competitions that have been around a long time have garnered respect from the film industry because they've earned it. Wins (or placements) in one of these competitions has the potential to generate quite a bit of interest in the writers and their scripts because the competition is so highly respected. Agents, managers, and producers eagerly await the results of these competitions because they want to know which scripts those competitions deemed "the best."

For example, Nicholl has garnered so much respect over the years that being a Nicholl semifinalist might generate more interest from the industry than winning a lesser-known competition.

Whether the competition promotes their winning/placing scripts or not, what ultimately matters is whether the competition's alumni end up with successful screenwriting careers.

All this said, the highly respected competitions often receive *thousands* of entries. So, even though winning or placing in those competitions could do a lot for your career, the odds of a script *reaching* that point are incredibly small. For example, for the 2018 competition year:

- AFF received 9,707 submissions (across all script formats/genres/categories) and awarded fifteen winners.

- Nicholl received 6,895 feature scripts and selected 4 winners.

- PAGE received 6,560 scripts (across all formats/genres/categories) and awarded one Gold, Silver, and Bronze winner in each format/genre/category plus one Grand Prize Winner.

Newer and lesser-known competitions typically receive far fewer submissions. So, while those competitions won't necessarily generate as much buzz, you might stand a better chance of placing or winning, which could be worth mentioning in a query or pitch.

Success Stories

Not only does a competition's "Success Stories" have the potential to help you determine the types of scripts the competition advances, those success stories can also help determine the degree to which winning (or placing) in the competition *directly affected the writer's career* (and in what way).

When I read success stories, I look for the following information:

1. The degree of success the winning (or placing) writers obtained. Did the writers garner agents or managers as a result of their competition success? Were they hired for any writing assignments? Has any of their work been produced?

2. Has the writer been hired, agented, etc.? If so, by whom?

3. Were any of the winning/placing *scripts* produced or optioned? If produced, by whom and how successfully?

4. Are the competition *winners* the only ones to receive any success? Or do those who place achieve success as well (and if so, at what tier did they place: quarterfinals, semifinals, finals, etc.)?

5. How much time typically passes between a writer's win/placement in the competition and the success that writer achieves?

6. How recent are the success stories? Have any of the writers who won/placed in the past five years shown career advancement?

None of these questions/answers are *guarantees* that if I win or place in the competition I'll have the same success. However, the answers give me an idea of how successful a competition is at helping a screenwriter get noticed by the industry.

Seeking Information

If you're new to screenwriting competitions, or unsure if you and/or your script are ready to win, then it might be best to enter competitions that give you the most insight into how your script *ranks* and/or those that provide written critiques.

Rank

As discussed earlier in *Screenplay Competitions*, not all competitions provide particulars regarding how your script ranked. Some competitions might announce nothing more than the winning scripts. That's it. Either you win or you don't. And that's the only information you get.

However, competitions that announce multiple advancement tiers (and provide corresponding entry/advancement numbers/percentages) provide greater insight regarding how a script ranked. Even if you don't win these competitions, you'll get some idea of how close you came and where among all the other entries your script stacked up.

That said, most competitions' first advancement tier comprises a very small percentage of the entered scripts—typically only the top 10% to 15%. If your script does *not* reach that first tier, you'll have no idea where among the other 85% or 90% of entries your script ranked.

Given this, it can be helpful to enter competitions where the initial advancing tier is made up of a larger percentage of entries (for example, the quarterfinalists for the ScreenCraft Sci-Fi and Fantasy Contest consist of the top 25% of entries).

This can be helpful because scripts that consistently reach the top 25% in multiple competitions typically require a different level of revision than scripts that consistently rank in the top 10%.

When one of my scripts consistently makes the top 10% it means the script is pretty solid and has the potential to place highly in competitions that award that type of script.

If my script consistently makes the top 25%, but rarely (or never) makes it any further, that is usually an indicator that I've demonstrated adept writing skills in many areas of screenwriting—but not in *all* areas of screenwriting. While the script is likely on the right track, it requires a few substantial rewrites to reach the next level (e.g. maybe I need to make the protagonist more layered, heighten the stakes of the plot, or streamline the exposition).

When a script consistently fails to make the top 25%, then odds are the writer needs to better familiarize him/herself with the screenwriting craft as a whole or that the individual script needs a lot of work. This doesn't mean the entire project needs to be tossed aside, but the writer will likely need to come at the story from a different angle. In other words, it's time to go back to the outlining stages and see where the story falls short.

Of course, when a competition's quarterfinals are made up of a large number of scripts, then reaching those quarterfinals likely won't generate any industry interest since the advancing scripts haven't been narrowed down enough. But if the competition's higher advancement tiers represent smaller numbers then reaching those tiers could still generate interest in your script.

Another way to glean insight into how your script ranks is to enter competitions that provide entrants with the number of rounds their scripts progressed through and/or provide entrants with the actual *scores* assigned to their scripts by their competition judges (scores assigned per judging criteria can be even more helpful). See "Determining Advancement" in Chapter 6 for more information.

Finally, and quite importantly, do not place too much emphasis on the ranking your script receives from just *one* competition—or, quite honestly, even from two or three. If you find your script ranks at a consistent level across *multiple* competitions, however, that is probably a reliable indication of the quality of your script and the amount of work the script might require.

Written Critiques

If competitions don't give you enough insight into how your script ranked in the competition, or if you need help determining the strengths and weaknesses of your script, then it might be beneficial to consider written critiques.

I discussed critiques in detail in Section III, so I won't go over it again here. Just remember that there are several types of critiques available to fit your writing needs, and it's in your best interest to always get more than one critique.

Section VI

The Submission Process

After you complete your research and have selected the competitions you want to enter, the next step is the actual submission process.

This section covers some of the more common aspects of the screenwriting competition submission process—what you'll likely encounter, and what you'll typically need when it comes time to submit.

17

Submission Dates and Deadlines

Before you begin the submission process, you need to determine *when* you can actually enter the competition.

Entry Dates

Typically, a competition is held annually with its entry and announcement dates falling on or around the same dates each year. But that's not always the case. So, I find it useful to look ahead and record the various entry dates associated with the competitions I want to enter for the upcoming competition year.

Open Date

The *open date* is the first day the competition starts accepting entries for that competition year.

Some competitions start accepting entries a few days after they announce the winners of the previous competition, and other competitions don't open until months after the previous year's results are announced.

Entry Period

A competition's entry period encompasses the span of time between the date and time a competition begins accepting entries and the date and time the competition stops accepting entries. Typically, entry periods last a few weeks to several months.

Entry Deadlines

Most competitions divide the entry period into multiple deadlines, the entry fee increasing after each deadline passes.

The entry fee often increases about $10 to $20 per deadline. Typically, the longer the entry period, the more entry deadlines. If a competition's entry period lasts only two months, it might only have two entry deadlines; but if the competition's entry period extends over six months, it might have five entry deadlines. For example:

ENTRY PERIOD	ENTRY FEE
January 1st through January 31st	$39
February 1st through February 28th	$49
March 1st through March 31st	$59

Entering a competition early can offer a financial advantage. If you're entering several competitions and/or several scripts, the savings can add up. Does that mean you *should* enter early just to save on the fee? Not necessarily—especially if your script isn't ready. Entering early when your script isn't ready means that you could end up wasting the entire entry fee, either because the script won't advance as far in the competition or because the critique you receive (if applicable) won't be as helpful since the critique will likely point out issues in your script that you were already aware of but didn't have time to fix.

However, if you think your script *is* ready for entry (or you know you won't be working on it anymore before the final entry deadline), then it makes sense to take advantage of the less expensive early entry fee.

It should be noted that in some rare cases, competitions allow you to *purchase* your entry early in their entry period at the less expensive entry fee but allow you to *submit your script* at any point after that during the entry period. This can be a money saver if you *know* you're going to submit your script by the final entry deadline. However, if you're not sure you'll be able to finish writing (or editing) your script by the final entry deadline, then you risk wasting the entire entry fee if it isn't refundable.

Final Entry Deadline

The final entry deadline is the final date the competition accepts entries.

The terminology each competition uses for their final entry deadline varies. For example, the last opportunity to enter your script might be called the "final entry deadline," the "late entry deadline," the "last minute deadline," or something else entirely. Whatever the competition calls it, this deadline is your last opportunity to enter your script in their competition for that competition year.

Even if something out of your control prevents your entry from being finalized by that final deadline, it's unlikely the competition will allow you to submit your entry once the deadline has passed.

Given that, I would advise *against* waiting until the final moments to enter a competition.

In fact, many competitions encourage you to enter *at least* a few days before the final deadline. This is primarily because (for online submissions) the competitions receive so many entries at the last minute that they cannot guarantee their submission systems won't crash. If the system does crash, or if the system is so overloaded that your entry doesn't get processed, the competition might *not* allow you to submit later.

Of course, it might not always be the competition's system that prevents your entry from being submitted on time. Other situations could include a power outage, your computer crashing, your Internet going out, or life in general getting in the way of your planned schedule.

It's also not ideal to wait until the last minute to mail submissions and/or payments or to phone in your payment. Things get lost in the mail and phone lines go down.

Now, if you *need* those last days or hours to really improve your script (and thus your chances of advancing in the competition), then you must decide if it's worth the risk to push your entry to the deadline.

Entry Times

Another important aspect of entry deadlines is not only the *date* but the *time* and the time *zone* of the deadline.

Is the deadline at 11:59 p.m. Pacific Standard Time? Or 5:00 p.m. Eastern Standard Time? Always check.

Additionally, make sure you understand if the deadline is on or *before* the date and time specified by the competition. Some competitions are very clear: "The final deadline is on January 15, 2019 at 11:59 p.m. Pacific Standard Time." But not all competitions are as specific: "The deadline is March 31st." Does that mean the deadline is on the 31st or that the entry must be submitted *before* the 31st? If it's not clear, I assume the submission must be completed the day *before*.

Keeping Records

You could keep revisiting a competition's website to remind yourself of the entry dates, times and fees. However, I find it easier to record this information for each of the competitions I plan to enter.

I keep track of competition entry-related dates, deadlines and fees on a spreadsheet. I also put the information in the calendar on my smartphone and add it to that old-fashioned thing: the wall calendar.

The spreadsheet allows me to sort by date, competition, or date-type (opening, first deadline, final deadline, etc.). The smartphone calendar gives me access to the information whenever and wherever (and I can set up alerts and reminders days or weeks in advance of a deadline). The wall calendar allows me to see at a glance the approaching deadlines.

Since each competition uses different terminology to refer to their various deadlines, for my own records, I mark each deadline with its corresponding number (e.g. "1 of 3" or "4 of 5"). This way I can identify which deadline is approaching and how many (if any) deadlines remain once that deadline passes.

All this can take a little time to do, but it's a fraction of the time I've spent writing my scripts and researching competitions. So, why not take a few steps to help alleviate the risk of missing out on a deadline and thus your opportunity to enter the competitions you selected?

18

Fees and Payment

Competitions cost money to enter. And most of us, by financial necessity, have to choose which competitions are most deserving of our dollars.

In trying to choose the best competitions for you and your script, know that the entry fee is only one piece of the puzzle. It's important to take every aspect of the competition into consideration. How many judges will judge your script in the first round? Will you receive a written critique? Is the critique included in the entry fee or a separate fee? Will the critique be thorough and criteria-specific? How many critiques will you receive? How effective do you think the competition will be at promoting your script if you win or place? Do you receive any prizes if you don't win but reach the finals? What about the semifinals or quarterfinals?

Obviously, there's a lot to consider and much depends on what you hope to garner from the competition experience and your honest evaluation of the strengths and weaknesses of your script. But money is a factor, so this chapter gives a quick rundown of the typical fees associated with entering competitions.

Fees

Usually, all fees related to an entry are required *at the time of submission or shortly thereafter*. Moreover, an entry won't be considered complete until the script, submission materials, *and payments* are received by the competition.

Entry Fee

The entry fee is the cost to actually enter a script in a competition. As I write this today, most entry fees range from $40 to $90 depending on the competition and entry deadline. The entry fee for teleplays and/or short scripts will typically be $5 to $10 less than a competition's entry fee for feature scripts.

Multiple Entries

Some competitions offer discounts on entry fees if you enter more than one script into the competition *at the same time*—not the following day or even the following hour, but during the same submission process (or in the same submission envelope).

Although this savings can be helpful, if you have one script ready for entry, but are still working on a second one, it might *not* be financially beneficial to *wait* to enter both your scripts simultaneously since the entry fee might increase (if an entry deadline passes) more than the multiple entry discount would save you.

Multiple Genres/Categories

In order to submit your script in more than one genre or category for judging, some competitions require you to submit the script *as an entirely new entry for each genre/category*.

For other competitions, you can enter the script under one genre/category (which is covered by the main entry fee), then you can add additional genres/categories for additional fees (but these fees are less than the main entry fee).

Multiple Judges

Some competitions that require only one first-round judge to advance or eliminate a script will provide entrants with the *option* to have their script evaluated and ranked by more than one judge *in that first round*. This usually comes with a fee, but it is often less expensive than the regular entry fee.

Be aware, however, that if you choose this option, and more than one first-round judge advances your script, your script will likely *not* be judged as separate entries for the following rounds. This is because your script is not being *entered* into the entire competition twice, you're just upping your odds of finding a judge who will advance your script from the first round to the second round.

Critique Fees

Many competitions offer some sort of written critique in conjunction with their competition. Some critiques are included with the entry fee and some cost an additional fee.

I discussed critique fees in Section III, so feel free to refer back for more detail. But, to recap, if you want to request/purchase a critique, you'll typically need to do so *at the time of entry* (though some competitions do allow entrants to purchase/request critiques after entry).

Finally, if the critique you've selected costs money, you'll likely need to pay for that critique at the same time you pay for your script entry.

Extra Page Fees

Some competitions charge a fee for scripts that exceed a specified page count. This could be a flat fee (e.g. any script over 120 pages will be charged an additional $10) or it could be a per page fee (e.g. $5 for each page over 120 pages). *Be sure to find out if the competition includes the title page in the page count.*

Print versus Online Fees

Some of the competitions that allow both online and mailed submissions will charge a small fee for one method over the other.

Shipping Costs

If you're mailing any part of your submission, remember to have the funds available to cover the shipping cost. You may also need a self-addressed stamped postcard, if requested by the competition, so they can confirm receipt of your mailed submission.

Penalty Fees

If your payment fails to process due to lack of funds, you may be charged a penalty fee. Moreover, your script/s may be disqualified from the competition.

Discounts

In addition to the savings some competitions offer for multiple entries and/or entry in multiple genres/categories, some competitions offer *other* types of discounts or savings relative to your entry. Here are some of the more common savings opportunities:

Promotional Discounts

Sometimes competitions offer promotions for discounted (or free) entries and/or critiques. Usually these promotions are announced on the competition's website, social media sites, and/or via email. Normally I see these promotions around the time the competition opens for entries or around event dates (e.g. Black Friday, Cyber Monday, the competition's anniversary).

Discounts on Other Services or Products

During the submission process, you may be presented with a discount on other services or products the competition organization provides if you purchase them at the time you enter their competition (e.g. written critiques, coverage, educational books, festival passes).

Student and Youth Discounts

Competitions may offer discounts to students and/or entrants under the age of 18. Typically, this is a savings benefit to the entrant and does not mean that his/her script will be judged any differently. However, some competitions do have special judging/award categories *for* students or minors.

If you plan to use these discounts, be sure you qualify. Do you need to be under the age of 18 on the date you enter or during the entire competition process? What qualifies you as a student? Is the discount for high school students only? College students? Do you have to be enrolled in film classes?

Thank You Discounts

Sometimes you'll receive discounts as a thank you from a competition you've already entered. These might be savings on the following year's competition (e.g. a free or discounted entry) or discounts on other services or products the competition organization provides (e.g. written critiques, coverage, educational books, festival passes). Typically this discount information will be sent to you via email.

Payment Method

Most competitions accept credit card payments (usually Visa and Mastercard, sometimes American Express and Discover®), some accept PayPal payments, and some accept checks or money orders.

Most competitions require payment to be made online, but a few will accept payment over the phone and/or through the mail. Additionally, most competitions held in the United States require payments to be made in U.S. funds.

19

Multiple Entries and Versions

While many competitions don't preclude entrants from submitting multiple scripts per competition year, or even multiple versions of a script... some competitions do.

Multiple Entries

It's pretty rare for competitions to cap the number of scripts you can enter per competition year. But it does happen. Nicholl, as discussed before, allows entrants to enter no more than three scripts per competition year.

It should be noted, however, that when competitions do allow multiple entries, it's unlikely entrants would be required to enter all the scripts *at the same time*.

If a competition allows writers to enter multiple scripts per competition year, it does not automatically mean that the competition will accept multiple *versions* of a script per competition year.

Multiple Versions

Some competitions do *not* allow entrants to submit more than one version of a script per competition year, and if you try to do so (say submit different versions under different titles), all your scripts could be disqualified.

If the competition *does* allow multiple versions of a script to be entered in the same competition year, then each version of the script would be treated as a separate entry and you'll be required to pay the associated entry fee for each version you submit, resulting in the two versions of your script competing with each other.

If you plan to submit multiple versions of a script, you might consider giving each version a slightly different title so you can identify how each version ranked. However, if your title is important to the script, then you might not want to risk changing it.

Resubmissions

A few competitions (like BlueCat and Scriptapalooza) allow you to submit a new version of your script as a *resubmission*. A fee is usually associated with this process, but it is typically less than the entry fee. In many cases the resubmitted script must be received before the competition's final entry deadline (or another specified date) and will be judged *in addition* to the originally submitted script—each version judged as its own unique entry.

Some competitions *encourage* resubmissions. For example, they will send you a written critique of your entered script within a month or so of your original entry so that (if you entered early enough during the entry period) you have time to receive that critique, make rewrites, and send your revision as a resubmission. BlueCat offers a process like this.

When entering your resubmission, you may need to reference the entry number the competition assigned to the original version of your script. Moreover, depending on the competition and judge availability, you may have the option to request the same judge who read the original version of your script.

Updated Versions

Many competitions provide entrants the opportunity to submit an updated version of their scripts when the entrants advance to a certain level within the competition (e.g. semifinalists or finalists). This revised script is usually judged *only* for the remaining rounds of competition (the previous rounds' rankings remain unchanged). There is no fee to do this (as it's a perk of reaching the corresponding advancement tier) and submitting the updated version is an *option*, not a *requirement*.

So, *should* you submit your revised script? On one hand, if your script made it to the final round/s of the competition, you may not want to tamper with a version that's being well received. On the other hand, if you've made changes to the script that you believe improve it significantly, then you might determine it's worthwhile to submit the newer version.

Incorrect Drafts/Versions

Usually, once you submit your script, that's it—no do-overs. Even if you realize immediately after you hit "submit" that the script you uploaded was the wrong draft, you probably won't be allowed to rectify the error.

Some competitions are more lenient than others and will let you submit the correct version if you contact the competition shortly after finalizing your entry and ask if you can send the correct draft (though a fee may be incurred). But, usually, entered is entered, and there's not much you can do about it.

However, *if* the competition allows resubmissions and/or entries of multiple versions of the same script (and if you realize your mistake while the entry period is still open and/or resubmissions are still accepted) then you can choose to enter the correct draft of your script *as a new entry or resubmission*.

Of course, if the competition caps the number of entries you're allowed per year and you've already maxed that out, then you wouldn't be able to enter a new version of your script as a new entry, even if multiple versions of scripts are allowed.

Bottom line: *be very careful* that you're submitting the correct version or draft of your script.

20

Submission Pathways

Most competitions require entrants to submit online. However, a few competitions do still accept mailed entries. Additionally, some competitions allow entrants to submit scripts online, but send payments through the mail. Or the other way around. Or pay over the phone. This chapter explores these processes.

Sending Scripts and Payments Separately

Before I delve into the various ways you can send submissions, I want to point out that submissions and payments don't always happen simultaneously (even if the entire submission process occurs online, it's common for the script-entry process to be separate from the payment process).

It's very important to know that *an entry isn't final until all submission materials and fees have been sent to and received by the competition*. This includes, not just the script and fees, but also any additional submission materials required (entry form, logline, etc.).

Just because you've received a confirmation of your *script submission* does not mean that the script is entered in the competition. Be sure you receive confirmation of *both* your script submission *and* payment.

You must also determine if the entry deadline and corresponding fees pertain to the submission of the script, the submission of the payment, or both.

For example, let's say the competition's entry deadline is January 15th at 11:59 p.m. Pacific Standard Time. You submit your script online by January 15th but don't mail your payment until January 20th. Will your entry be disqualified? Do you pay the January 15th entry fee or the January 20th entry fee? What if you post the payment on the 15th but the competition doesn't receive it until the 20th? What if the 15th was the *final* entry deadline?

If the competition doesn't clearly address these questions, contact them for clarification.

Online Systems

While the online submission process is similar from one competition to the next (fill out an entry form, upload a PDF of your script, pay with a credit card), you will come across different types of online submission pathways.

Online Store

To accept submissions, some competitions use their website and corresponding online store. You complete the entry form and upload your script (and any additional materials) on their site. Then you add your submission to their shopping cart and go through the "check-out" process to submit payment, thus finalizing your entry.

Account

Some competitions require you to create an account through their website in order to enter your script in their competition. You'll typically use this account to not only submit your script (and often payment as well), but also to monitor your script's submission status and access any applicable critiques. Given this, you will need to keep a record of your login and password for the account. Moreover, you'll likely need to use the same account (same login and password) for future submissions for that competition year and/or future competition years.

If you must register, you may be required to agree to the terms and conditions and privacy policies of the organization's entire website. This fine print can be a great deal longer and more tedious to read than the competition's fine print, so make sure you leave plenty of time for this additional reading.

Third-Party Submission Source

Sometimes a competition will utilize a third-party submission source (e.g. Coverfly, FilmFreeway, Submittable). These third-party sources may require you to create an account with them before you can start the submission process.

If you use these sources, make sure you read and understand their fine print in addition to the competition's. This can be very time consuming, so I suggest you make a list of the third-party submission sources used by the competitions you want to enter. Determine if any *one* of those third-party sources is used by *all* the competitions you want to enter (or at least all the competitions that require you to use a third-party submission source). If so, read that submission source's fine print and, if you're okay agreeing to that fine print, use that one source for all your third-party submissions (instead of having to read the fine print of *multiple* third-party submission sources).

Competition Website with Third-Party Payment Source

Many competitions require you to submit your script, entry form, and any additional materials through the competition's website. When you click "submit," you will be taken to another web page that will allow you to start the payment process.

Often the payment process is handled through a third-party (like PayPal). Because of this, after you submit your script, but before you've started the payment process, you'll probably be taken to a "submission confirmation" page that contains a link to the payment processing page. Be aware that even though your *submission* has been confirmed you still need to *pay* for the submission in order for it to be finalized.

Once you've submitted your script, submission materials, and paid for the submission, you should receive two email confirmations: one from the payment processor confirming your payment and the other from the competition confirming your submission. You might receive a third email from the competition confirming that your entry fee was received and your script's entry in the competition was finalized.

Payment via Mail or Phone

Some competitions allow you to submit your entry through their website and then pay via phone or by sending a check through the mail. When this happens, you'll likely need to include a copy of your completed entry form and/or submission confirmation with your payment (if sent through the mail) or have the submission confirmation number ready (if paying over the phone).

Online Confirmations

If you've processed any part of your submission online then you should receive two types of confirmations:

1. A *web page* that confirms your script and/or payment submission was successful (which I suggest you print or save as a PDF or screenshot).

2. An *email* that confirms your script and/or payment submission was successful (which I also suggest you save).

Confirmation emails are usually sent immediately after submission, but not always. Typically competitions will specify when you can expect to receive confirmation emails so you know when to follow up with the competition if the confirmations don't arrive.

If the competition uses a third-party (for script submission and/or payment) then you should receive confirmations *from that third-party*. You'll likely *also* receive confirmations directly from the competition.

Remember: It's important to make sure you receive confirmations for *both* script submission and payment. Whether these come in one email or two, if you don't receive email confirmations for both, then I suggest contacting the competition.

Mail

If you submit your *script* online but are mailing *payment*, you will likely need to print the completed online entry form and include it and/or the script submission confirmation with your payment—this way, competition organizers can match your payment to your script.

If you *paid* online (or over the phone) and are mailing your script, you will likely need to include your completed entry form with the script, as well as the payment confirmation.

If you're mailing any aspect of your submission, find out if the entry deadline pertains to the date the submission is *mailed* (postmarked) or the date the competition *receives* it. If mailing your payment, does the competition require your payment funds to clear by the deadline?

If you're entering multiple scripts (or multiple versions of the same script) find out if each entry needs its own submission envelope. Similarly, if you're mailing payment for more than one entry, find out if the payments can be combined (on the same check/money order and/or in the same submission envelope).

Make sure you select the carrier (e.g. UPS®, United States Postal Service®, FedEx®) and shipping method (e.g. ground, priority) that the competition specifies.

If you have a choice, I suggest you select a shipping method that offers tracking and *guarantees* delivery by the required deadline.

However, just because a shipper guarantees delivery by a specific date does not ensure that the delivery will be delivered by that date. Mail gets lost, packages get misrouted, things happen. So mail your submission materials/payment with enough time for the competition to receive and process them—and (ideally) so you have enough time remaining to submit again in the event your original submission is not received.

Some competitions allow you to include a self-addressed, stamped postcard with your mailed submission which they return to you as confirmation of receipt of your submission (script and/or payment). If the competition doesn't accept confirmation postcards, find out if you should expect a confirmation email instead.

Phone

While you can't submit your script over the phone, some competitions allow you to pay your entry fees over the phone. If you pay over the phone, find out if you should receive a payment confirmation number, and/or if you should expect a payment confirmation email.

Not only is the confirmation important for your own records, but you might need to reference the payment confirmation number when you submit your script.

If you already submitted your script (by mail or online), you might need the script's submission confirmation number when you phone to pay for the submission so that competition organizers can match your payment to your script entry.

Finally, if you're going to pay by phone, make sure you allow enough time to actually reach the office before the deadline. Is the office closed on weekends? Holidays? What if the line is busy at the last minute because they are flooded with other entrants trying to pay?

21

What You Will Need for Submission

Following is a list of what you will typically need when it comes time to submit your entry.

An Understanding of the Fine Print

Always, always, always read the fine print. Know what you're agreeing to. Yes, it's dull, it's repetitive, and it's challenging, but please do it. Read through the competition's guidelines, eligibility requirements, rules, terms and conditions, privacy policies, frequently asked questions, agreements, prizes, awards, commitments, etc. Be sure you are comfortable adhering to and agreeing to all of it.

Moreover, you need to know if entering, winning, placing, or advancing in the competition in any way changes your rights to your script.

Allow enough time to read (and digest) everything before you enter. I know this can be stressful and tedious. But you've put months, or years, into your script, so take the necessary time and read what's going to happen to it after you hit *submit*.

Besides, it's important to get comfortable reading legalize. The more legalize you read, the easier it is to understand.

Finally, when possible, save copies of the fine print (print it, save it as screenshots, save PDFs, etc.).

Time

Once you start the submission process, rarely can you save your progress and complete the submission later. A few competitions provide this luxury, but not many. So set aside enough time to get through the entire submission process in one sitting.

I suggest you set aside *at least* an hour to complete the submission process, longer for the first few times you enter a competition. And that's *provided* you've done all the prep work ahead of time (formatted your script, the title page, written your logline, read through all the rules and fine print, etc.).

An hour might seem like a lot, but even if you read through the fine print available to you *prior* to starting the submission process, when it comes time to actually submit your script, you'll likely be taken to web pages that you didn't have access to before, and those pages usually contain more fine print that you will be required to read and agree to prior to clicking submit.

Lastly, if you need to read the fine print of the actual competition organization's website (especially for those competitions that require registration), or if you need to use a third-party submission source (and thus need to read their fine print), then I suggest you take a look at that fine print a good week before you're ready for submission so you know how much reading you'll have to do since that fine print can be 20, 30, 40 pages or more.

Funds

You will need to have funds available *at the time* you enter your script, or shortly thereafter, to cover your entry fees and any other purchases you've added during the submission process (e.g. written critiques or festival passes).

Critique Decision

As discussed earlier, most competitions that offer competition-related critiques require you to make that purchase/request *at the time you enter the competition*.

This doesn't mean they require you to purchase a critique, but rather that *if* you're going to purchase the critique, you typically must make that selection (and payment) at the time you submit your script.

Given this, it's a good idea to decide *prior* to starting the entry process if you plan to request/purchase a critique.

Your Script

If you plan to mail a physical copy of your script, make sure you follow the competition's formatting requirements (page size, title page cardstock, number of brads, whether pages can be double-sided, etc.).

For electronic submissions, your script needs to be in an accepted file type. Most competitions accept PDFs, but a few competitions accept other files types, like Word documents, Final Draft® or Movie Magic®. There are often size limits to the file you can upload and restrictions regarding locked and/or password protected files, etc. Competitions usually want the script's file name to be either the title of your script or title and author name.

Whether the script is sent through the mail or sent electronically, competitions usually do *not* want you to include your name or any personally identifying information anywhere *within the body of the script* (even if it's allowed on the title page—discussed next).

Finally, competitions do not return scripts or other submission materials. This isn't as big an issue when you're submitting materials electronically, but if you're planning to mail your script/submission materials, be sure to retain a copy (or, preferably, *multiple* copies) for yourself.

Title Page

Some competitions require your script's title page to include *just* the script's title. Others require title and author name/s. If a script has multiple writers/contributors then each competition has different requirements regarding how those writers/contributors should be referenced on the title page. Some competitions require title, author name/s *and* author contact information. A few competitions request the title page to also include the script's logline and/or genre. And finally, most competitions will allow (though don't require) your copyright and/or Writer's Guild of America registration numbers to be included on the title page.

It can be tedious to continually open a script and change the title page every time you enter a competition. And, personally, I'm always a little terrified I'll accidently change something in the body of the script. So, to avoid confusion (and to lower my stress levels) I save multiple files of my finished script—the only difference between them being the information included on the title page.

Now, I *could* give each of these scripts a file name that distinguishes its title page. For example, suppose I wrote a script titled *Next Best Screenplay.* I could save the various files as:

- Next Best Screenplay title only
- Next Best Screenplay title and name
- Next Best Screenplay title name and contact
- Next Best Screenplay title and genre

This seems simple enough at first—except that competitions usually want the script's file name to be the script's title and that's it.

Given this, if I want to avoid having to constantly rename the file I'm going to upload, I create *folders* to identify the title page for each saved copy of my script and move the script files to those respective folders.

When all is said and done, I end up with a filing system like this:

1. A "Next Best Screenplay" folder.

2. Within that folder is a submissions subfolder for that calendar year, e.g. "Next Best Screenplay 2020 Submissions".

3. Within the "Next Best Screenplay 2020 Submissions" folder is a subfolder for *each* title page configuration. So, I have *subfolders* labeled:

   - Next Best Screenplay title only
   - Next Best Screenplay title and name
   - Next Best Screenplay title name and contact
   - Next Best Screenplay title and genre

4. Then I move the corresponding *script files* to those appropriately labeled subfolders.

This way, each script file can be labeled "Next Best Screenplay" and when it comes time to upload my script, the folders make it easy to locate the script file with the appropriate title page.

Of course, this is just my system. You will find a system that works for you, and that's what's important.

Copyright and/or Registration

Most competitions don't require you to copyright or register your script prior to entering their competitions. But most competitions strongly *advise* that you do.

I copyright all my scripts with the United States Copyright Office. But writers can register their work with the Writer's

Guild of America instead. Or do both. Just allow enough time to complete this process before your entry deadlines.

It can take several months for your material to be fully copyrighted/registered. So keep records of your copyright/registration submission, case number, and your payment receipt. Then you can prove the date you submitted your script for copyright/registration and that you paid the accompanying fees. If you decide to enter competitions before you receive the official copyright/registration at least you have some proof of ownership.

Entry Form

When it comes time to actually submit your script to the competition you will be required to complete an entry form (or "submission form," "application form," "registration form," etc.). This is typically a form on the competition's website (ranging from one to multiple pages). Some competitions do provide paper forms (though these may need to be printed from their website).

The information required to complete the entry form pertains to you and your script (each discussed shortly). Typically, the information will be entered directly onto the entry form, though sometimes it will need to be attached. For example, if the competition requires a short writer biography then that might be entered onto the entry form or attached as a separate document. If you're submitting electronically, check that any attachments are in file types the competition accepts. If you're submitting through the mail, then the additional materials will likely need to be included in the same envelope as the rest of your submission (though check if the competition wants any of the submission materials physically attached to each other, and if so, what type of fastener they require).

If you submit your entry form online but send part of your submission through the mail, you might be required to print your completed entry form and include it with your submission envelope.

Script Information

Competitions need to gather information about each script entered in their competition. What follows is some of the common script information requested on entry forms.

- ***Script Format***. If the competition you are entering accepts more than one script format then you'll need to identify the format of your particular script (e.g. feature script or teleplay).

- ***Script's Genre/s***. You will likely need to specify your script's genre/s, even if the competition doesn't utilize genre-specific judging.

- ***Page Count***. You may be required to indicate your script's page length.

- ***Adaptations or True/Historical Events***. If your script is an adaptation or based on true/historical events, then some competitions require you to identify this at the time of entry. You might also be required to submit (either at time of entry or later) proof that you hold the rights to the adaptation/story and/or that it is in the public domain.

- ***Loglines/Summaries***. Write your logline/summary in advance of entering competitions so that you have enough time to make it as captivating, compelling, and succinct as possible. Not only will this help get your script into the hands of judges who are most likely to appreciate it, but if your script wins or places well in the competition, this logline/summary might be used to promote your script. And while winning or placing in a competition is a first step to gaining interest from individuals in the industry, the second step is very often your script's logline or summary. Therefore, it should be representative of your story and captivating enough to make industry professionals want to *request your complete script*.

- ***Additional Materials***. Unless it's at the competition's request, do not send any additional materials with your entry. For example, unless the competition requests a writer biography, a summary of the script, ideas for casting, etc., do not send them. That said, for television pilot entries, some competitions do accept the corresponding standard supplementary materials (e.g. a list of recurring characters and/or a summary of future episodes).

Writer Information

Competitions need to gather information about their entrants. What follows is some of the common writer/contributor information requested on competition entry forms.

- ***Name and Contact Information***. You'll need to provide your name and contact information (address, email address, and phone number). Remember, this information might be distributed to individuals in the film industry who could be interested in contacting you regarding your script. Moreover, your name (and potentially contact information) will likely be included on any advancement announcements (if your script advances).

- ***Multiple Writers/Contributors***. If the script you enter has multiple writers and/or contributors, you'll be required to inform the competition of this upon entry. Usually only one writer will be the contact person for the competition (the person who receives confirmation emails, critiques, announcements, etc.). So, prior to starting the entry process, you and your fellow writers/contributors must decide who that contact person will be.

- ***Writer Biography or Letter***. At the time of entry or once you place at a specific tier, some competitions will request/require you to submit a biography or letter about yourself, your script, your writing aspirations, etc. The competition may specify the length required and provide guidelines for topics the bio/letter should cover. Sometimes these bio/letters are used as part of the judging process, and sometimes they are not. And sometimes they are used in advancement announcements if your script places highly enough.

- ***Competition Related Information***. Competitions may ask these types of questions: How did you hear about this competition? Have you entered this competition previously? Did you enter *this* script into this competition previously? Have any of your scripts placed in or won this competition in prior years? (Whether your answers are required or simply requested depends on the competition and the question).

Submission Records or Template

I highly suggest you keep track of your competition entries—which competitions you plan to enter, which competition you *do* enter, which scripts (and versions) you submit to each competition, which genres you submit under, etc.

I created a Submission Template for this purpose (which is discussed in Section VII). You don't *need* to use the Submission Template when entering competitions. However, I find that the Submission Template helps me keep track of not just which competitions I entered, but also how my script/s ranked once results are announced.

One Final Thought

The journey to a screenwriting career can be a long one with plenty of ups and downs. So take time to enjoy the good moments along the way (your personal beats, so to speak).

You finished your script. You entered a competition. You received a positive comment about your writing in a constructive critique. You made it past the first round, the second round. You're a quarterfinalist, a semifinalist, *a winner*!

Each of these moments can be sweet, but if you're only focused on winning, you might miss just how wonderful all these other moments can be.

Don't miss them. Savor them.

And most of all: enjoy writing.

Section VII

Templates

Section VII includes three templates:

1. The Competition Template

2. The Competition Round Template

3. The Submission Template

The Competition Template should be completed *per competition*. It is designed to help you identify key aspects of each competition that you research so you can better determine which competitions are a good match for you and your script.

The Competition Round Template should also be completed *per competition*. It is designed to help you identify and organize a competition's judging process so that you can decide, based on that process, if you want to enter the competition. And, for some competitions, the information in the completed Round Template can be useful when trying to determine exactly how far your script advanced in the competition, as well as the judging process used to get there.

The Submission Template should be completed *per year* and/or *per script per year* (whichever you prefer). This template is designed to help you keep track of your submissions and your results.

22

Using the Templates

You are welcome to use any of the three templates I've included in *Screenplay Competitions* or customize them for your own personal use.

It's important to realize that competitions don't always provide the information you need to fully complete these templates. So, if you come across a competition that interests you, my suggestion would be to complete the templates *to the best of your ability given the information the competition provides*. Then, if the competition still interests you, but you need further information, you can always contact the competition organizers and (hopefully) get the answers you need in order to make your final decision about whether to enter that competition or not.

I suggest you give these templates a test run to get used to them. To do that, visit the PAGE website and complete the templates as if you were going to enter the PAGE competition. I'm not saying you *should* or *should not* enter PAGE's competition, but PAGE's website (as I write this today) provides most of the data you'll need to complete the templates. Moreover, the data is easy to find and understand.

Once you've done that, I suggest you visit the Nicholl website and do the same thing. Again, I'm not saying you should or shouldn't enter the Nicholl competition, but Nicholl provides a lot of information on their website. However, it might take you a little longer to locate the information you're looking for (hint: be sure to check out their FAQs). Additionally, some of the information you seek might not be located directly on the Nicholl website—you might need to peruse their social media posts to find more.

Once you're comfortable with the templates, you can start using them for your own competition research. The more research you do, the more you'll find ways to customize the templates to fit your needs. And that's great! The fields I've included in these templates should apply to most scripts, writers, and competitions, but that doesn't mean you can't add your own fields—in fact, I encourage it!

Maybe you need to add some eligibility fields. Perhaps you've written an adaptation, so you need to add a field for competitions that accept adaptations. Maybe you've written a feature script that exceeds 120 pages, so you need a field to indicate if competitions accept feature scripts of your page count (and any associated fees for those extra pages). Perhaps you've earned money writing for the screen so you need a field to record a competition's earning requirements. Or, maybe you want to add some fields relative to what you hope to gain from the competition process (maybe you want to enter competitions with a higher percentage of quarterfinalists, or maybe you want to enter competitions that provide you with your script's score, or maybe you only want to enter fellowships).

Finally, don't rely solely on the information in your completed Competition or Round Templates for future years. Tedious as it is, you'll need to research a competition *each* time you enter, and update the templates with any changes from one competition year to the next.

The good news is, once you've done this a few times, you become better and quicker at it. And, hopefully, the record keeping involved will provide beneficial information for years to come.

23

The Competition Template

The Competition Template is the first template you'll use when you start researching competitions. It's a checklist of the key aspects of a competition. It is designed to help you narrow down which competitions you can and *want* to enter.

You will fill out this template per competition. Furthermore, if you have more than one format of script you want to enter (e.g. a teleplay *and* a feature script), then you can either complete this template *per format* or create separate columns for each format because eligibility requirements, judging processes, etc. could be different for each format.

The more you research competitions, the more this checklist will become second nature. Your reliance on it should lessen in the future. However, I do suggest you use the template if you are new to screenwriting competitions.

On the following page is a Competition Template completed for the fictionalized competition: "The 2020 Mock Screenplay Contest." While the competition is fabricated (as is the "entered script"), I've tried to keep the information similar to what you're likely to encounter when researching real competitions.

The Competition Template Example

Part A

The 2020 Mock Screenplay Contest	Competition Year: 2020
Formats Accepted: Feature Scripts. **Genres Accepted:** All Genres	

Part B

Enter Competition	Yes _√_ No___	**Reason:** Clear judging process
Script/s to Enter	The Next Great Screenplay	**Genre/s:** Drama and sci-fi

Part C

Entry Dates/Fees			
First		Jan 15, 2020 @ 11:59 p.m. PST $45	
Second		Feb 15, 2020 @ 11:59 p.m. PST $55	
Third		Mar 15, 2020 @ 11:59 p.m. PST $65	
Final		Apr 15, 2020 @ 11:59 p.m. PST $75	
Advancement Announcement Dates			
Quarterfinalists	7/15/2020	Online Post and Email	Score of 85+ from 1 judge or a combined score of 160+ from 2 judges
Semifinalists	8/15/2020	Online Post and Email	Top 5% per genre
Finalists	9/15/2020	Online Post (phone call to finalists)	Top 5 scripts per genre
Winners	10/15/2020	Online Post (phone call to winners)	1 overall winner, 1 winner per genre

Part D

Genre-Specific Judging	Yes
Genres Judged	10 genre categories including SciFi/Fantasy & Drama
Judging Criteria	Concept, Formatting, Plot, Structure, Characters, Dialogue, Overall
Judge Credentials	Professional Script Readers through Film Producers
Seeking Writers/Material	Yes. First round judges at least. Judge contacts writer after comp. ends

Part E

Number of Awards	1 Grand prize winner and 1 winner per genre (10 genres total).
Prizes	Grand Prize winner = $10,000. Genre winners = $500 each. All winners have their script title, logline, and contact info included in announcement book sent to the competition's list of agents, managers, and producers.

Part F

Previous Entry Numbers	2019: 6,895 total entries, 723 for sci-fi/fantasy, 1,941 for drama.

Part G

Number of Scripts Allowed	3 scripts per competition year
Multiple Versions of Script	Yes
Updated Versions	Yes, for finalists only. Must send within 10 days of finalist notifications
Resubmissions	Yes
Resubmission Deadline	Final entry deadline, April 15, 2020 @ 11:59 p.m. PST
Resubmission Fee	$25
Title Page	Title only
Logline/Summary	Logline required. Not used for judging. Used for promotion if script wins.
Writer Bio/Letter	No
Page Range	75 to 125 pages. Scripts under or over will be disqualified
Age of Script	No limit

Part H

Retain Rights	Yes
Agreements	Winners must send a verification of eligibility within 10 days of advancement announcement. Winners' script titles, loglines, and contact info will be distributed to 100 agents, managers, and producers. No options, sales, or production guarantees

Part I

Critique Terminology	Judge's Notes
Critique Fee	$45
Written By	First Round Judge in the competition
Critic Credentials	Professional Script Reader
Seeking Writers/Material	Yes. Critic contacts writer within 3 weeks of sending critique
Critique Receipt Date	After script is eliminated from (or wins) the competition
Number to be Received	1
Length	1 page
Content	Overall summary, includes judging criteria scores

The Competition Template Explained

The Competition Template has eight parts. What follows is an explanation of those parts and the their individual fields.

Part A

Part A exists to keep your records clear and easy to reference.

Competition Name. Enter the *full and complete* name of the competition including any yearly references. For example, The *2020* Mock Screenplay Contest.

By accurately listing the competition name, you'll have the name appropriately recorded in the event you want to reference a competition win/placement in your query letters or pitches.

Competition Year. Record the competition year in this field (not all competitions include the competition year in their competition name). The competition year may or may not be the year you *enter* the competition. It can apply to *either* the year the competition opens for entries or the year the competition announces winners. Accurately recording the year of the competition (as denoted by the competition) is important in case you want to reference a win/placement in a query or pitch.

Formats Accepted. Use this field to indicate which script formats the competition accepts (features, shorts, teleplays, a combination thereof). You can choose to add fields to address whether the competition accepts spec and/or shooting scripts. If you want to enter a teleplay, you might want to add a field to address if the competition accepts pilots and/or specs. Similarly, if the competition accepts spec teleplays, record any relative stipulations (e.g. the competition only accepts specs for shows that were currently airing new episodes as of the date the competition opened for entries).

Finally, if you write scripts in more than one format, then create a Competition Template per competition *per format* or create a *column* for each format.

Genres Accepted. Not all competitions accept all genres, so this field exists to record the genres a competition accepts that are *pertinent to the script/s you want to enter*.

If you've written a teleplay, then use this field to indicate how the competition categorizes teleplays (by length, by genre, or a combination of the two).

Finally, if the competition offers any unique judging categories that you'd like to enter your script under (e.g. "scripts with a female protagonist") then record those categories here.

Part B

Only complete Part B once you have decided to enter the competition (or not).

Enter Competition. Once you've decided if you do or do not want to enter the competition put a check mark in the appropriate spot.

Reason. Use this field to record your unique reasons for entering (or not entering) the competition. For example, if you decide to enter you might say, "critiques look helpful," or "excellent judging process." If you decide against entering, you might say, "doesn't accept dramas," or "doesn't announce any quarterfinalists."

Finally, if you really like a competition but your current script isn't eligible, then you might indicate that you would consider the competition in the future with an eligible script.

Script/s to Enter. List the script/s that you intend to enter in the competition.

Genre/s. Record the genre/s (and/or categories) you'll enter your script/s under (if applicable).

Part C

The fields in Part C are devoted to entry dates, entry fees, and announcement dates.

Entry Dates/Fees. Record the date, time, and time zone of the various deadlines. Also record the corresponding fee for each deadline. For example, the fee to enter The 2020 Mock Screenplay Contest on January 15th would be $45. However, if you wait to enter until January 16th the fee would be $55.

Advancement Announcement Dates. Record the competition's advancement tiers, what those tiers represent, and when the corresponding announcements will be made. You can also indicate *how* the announcement will be made (e.g. email, phone call, letter, online post).

Part D

Part D is devoted to the competition's judging process. You can be as detailed as you like. I've kept the information brief because the finer details of the judging process will be covered in the Competition Round Template. If you don't plan to use the Round Template, you might want to record more information here.

Genre-Specific Judging. Indicate here if the competition uses genre-specific (or format/category-specific) judging.

Genres Judged. If the competition uses genre-specific (or format/category-specific) judging, then record the total number here. Then record the genres (or formats/categories) you plan to enter your script under *as the competition categorizes them for judging* (e.g. comedy, drama, sci-fi/fantasy, thriller/horror).

Judging Criteria. If the competition provides their judging criteria, record it here. I find this helpful for two reasons:

1. Knowing a competition's judging criteria helps me select the competitions whose criteria suits my script. For example, if I've written a niche, indie script I might not want to enter the script in a competition that's looking for big-budget scripts.

2. Once I receive my script's results from various competitions, I review the corresponding judging criteria and decipher if there's any relationship between judging criteria and how my script ranked.

Judge Credentials. If you're going to use the Competition Round Template then you only need to enter a brief summary of judge credentials here (as I've done in the example Competition Template) because you'll use the Competition Round Template to enter judge credentials specific to each round of competition. However, if I were not going to use the Competition Round Template I would be more thorough here.

Seeking Writers/Material. Record if judges are actively seeking new writers and/or material and, if so, which rounds those judges evaluate. You could also record how and when you would be contacted if a judge is interested in your writing (e.g. by email after the competition winners are announced).

Part E

Part E exists so you can record the awards and prizes offered by the competition.

Number of Awards. Record the number of awards presented by the competition and the terminology used for those awards (e.g. winners, runners-up, bronze prize winners).

Prizes. Record the specific prizes offered by the competition per advancement/award level.

Part F

In Part F you will record entry numbers from the previous competition year/s.

Previous Entry Numbers. Record the total number of entries the competition received in prior years. While these numbers won't be representative of the entries the competition will receive in their current year, it will give you an idea of whether that competition receives hundreds of entries per year or *thousands* of entries per year.

If the competition uses format, genre, or category-specific judging, then also record the number of entries the competition received in the past for each of the formats, genres and/or categories you're considering entering.

If entry numbers aren't readily available on a competition's website, you can try searching for previous years' advancement announcements (since those sometimes include entry numbers) or search the competition's social media pages for posts during the prior competition years to see if any of those contain entry numbers.

Finally, if you decide to enter the competition, add a field for the *current* year's numbers so you can record those if/when the competition releases them.

Part G

Part G is for submission and eligibility requirements.

Number of Scripts Allowed. If the competition caps the number of scripts you can submit per competition year, then record that number here.

Multiple Versions of Script. Use this field to indicate if the competition allows you to submit more than one *version* of a script per competition year.

Updated Versions. Indicate whether the competition allows updated versions of scripts that reach a certain tier in the competition and, if so, the name of that tier (e.g. finalist tier). Also record when the updated script can be submitted.

Resubmissions. Indicate whether the competition allows resubmissions.

Resubmission Deadline. Enter the final date by which the competition must receive the resubmission.

Resubmission Fee. Record the fee associated with a resubmission.

Title Page. Record what the competition requests/requires on your script's title page.

Logline/Summary. Indicate if the competition requires a logline and/or summary with your submission and if either will be used for judging purposes and/or promotion if your script places in the competition. Also record any stipulations the competition makes regarding the content and length of your logline and/or summary.

Writer Bio/Letter. Indicate if the competition requires a writer biography and/or letter (either at the time of submission or if your script reaches a specified advancement tier). Indicate if that bio/letter will be used for judging purposes and/or promotion if your script places in the competition. Record any stipulations relative to the bio/letter's content and length.

Page Range. Enter the page length the competition accepts per script format. If your script does not fall within that range, record whether the script will be disqualified or charged an additional fee.

Age of Script. Some competitions won't accept submissions for scripts that were finished X-number of years prior to the current competition year or were submitted to a competition more than X-number of years ago. If that's the case, record those stipulations in this field.

Additional Fields. The fields I included in Part G should apply to any writer or script. However, you will likely need to customize this portion of the template. Review the eligibility requirements (Section IV) to help you determine which requirements pertain to you and your script. Add the necessary fields to customize your template. Here are some examples:

- **Adaptations**. Indicate if the competition accepts adaptations and, if so, if the competition requires any proof you own the rights to the adaptation.
- **Age of Writer**. This is especially important if you are under 18 years old.
- **Students**. Some competitions are exclusively for students, have student-specific award categories and/or offer discounts for students.
- **Earnings Limits**. Add this field if you have ever earned money writing endeavor—either being paid or through competition winnings.
- **Previous competition entries or wins**. Add this field for stipulations regarding if you've entered, placed in, or won this or another competition.
- **Rights/Ownership/Production**. If your script, or a version of it, has ever been bought, sold, produced, published, optioned, etc., add a field to address applicable eligibility requirements.
- **Multiple Writers/Contributors**. If you're not the sole writer/contributor of your script then add fields to record if the competition accepts entries by multiple writers/contributors as well as other pertinent information (e.g. if there's a limit to how many writers/contributors can be attached to a script, how those writers/contributors should be referenced on the script's title page and entry form, which of the writers/contributors will be the primary contact, and how the writers/contributors will allocate any prizes).

- **Fellowships**. If you've won any fellowships you'll need a field to indicate which competitions will still accept your entries.
- **Additional Materials**. If you wrote a television pilot, add a field to indicate if the competition accepts additional materials relative to that pilot and any stipulations regarding that material (e.g. only accepts a list of recurring characters).

Part H

Part H deals with the rights, ownership, and other fine print associated with entering a competition.

Retain Rights. Record if entrants retain all rights to their work whether they win the competition or not. If not, enter the specifics of how those rights might be affected. This would include option deals, first look clauses, guaranteed representation or production, etc.

Agreements. Record anything else you are agreeing to by entering, advancing in, placing in or winning the competition. Usually entrants will need to agree to let the competition use entrants' name, likeness, script title and logline, and reference any future successes. But there could be other agreements, too. Fellowships, for example, typically have obligations that winners must maintain or they risk forfeiting the fellowship.

Part I

Part I pertains to written critiques. If you have no interest in written critiques, then you can skip this portion.

If the competition (or related organization) does not offer

any written critiques, simply enter "None Offered" and ignore the rest of Part I.

If the competition (or related organization) you're researching offers *more* than one type of written critique, then you can duplicate this part of the template for each critique service that interests you.

Critique Terminology. Record the terminology the competition uses relative to the critique (e.g. Judge's Feedback, Reader Notes, General Comments).

Critique Fee. Record the cost of the critique. If the critique is included with your entry fee, simply enter "Included."

Written By. Indicate whether the critique will be written by your competition judge/s or not.

Critic Credentials. If the competition specifies the credentials required for their critics, record those credentials here. Or, if the critique is written by your script's competition judge/s you can enter "See Judge Credentials." If you later receive your critic's actual credentials with your critique you can update this field with that information.

Seeking Writers/Material. Record if the critics are actively seeking new writers and/or material. You could also add how and when you would be contacted if a critic is interested in your writing.

Critique Receipt Date. Record the date you can expect to receive your critique. Typically, it will be one of the following:

1. A specific or approximate *date*. For example, "January 1, 2020 by 12:00 p.m. PST" or "Early January".

2. An estimated time frame *following your entry and/ or critique request*. For example, 4-6 weeks after entry or 1-2 months from purchase.

3. An estimated time frame *after your script is eliminated from (or wins) the competition* and the corresponding announcement has been made. For example, 2-3 weeks after elimination or a week after winners have been announced.

Knowing when you will receive your critique is important if you plan to make rewrites based on those critiques prior to entering other competitions (and so you can contact a competition in case you don't receive your critiques when expected).

Number to be Received. Record the number of critiques you will receive with your request/purchase. If the number depends on how far your script advances in the competition, then enter the *minimum* number you'll receive followed by "more if script advances." Once you receive your critiques, you can always go back and record the exact number you received.

Length. Record how long critique/s should be (e.g. one paragraph, one page, 4-7 pages).

Content. Record a summary of what the critique will cover. For example, "an overall summary" or "detailed analysis, judging criteria scores, pass/consider/recommend, and log-line."

24

The Competition Round Template

The Competition Round Template is designed to help you better understand a competition's judging and advancement process. To do this, complete one template *per* round of a competition.

Remember, a round is not necessarily the same as an advancement tier, since a competition can have more than one set of script advancements/eliminations (rounds) per tier (e.g. quarterfinals, semifinals, finals).

I discussed the Competition Round Template in Chapter 7 so I won't repeat the information here. The following pages include completed Competition Round Templates for all five rounds of The 2020 Mock Screenplay Contest.

Though the competition is entirely fabricated, I've incorporated aspects of real competitions to give you an idea of what you're likely to encounter during your research.

That said, it is rare to come across a competition that will provide enough information to complete *all* the fields of this template for *all* rounds of their competition. So, complete the template as thoroughly as you can based on the information supplied by the competition. Then decide if that information (combined with the information you recorded on the Competition Template) is enough to make a decision on whether you want to enter the competition.

Finally, some of the Competition Round Template fields can only be completed *after* you enter the competition and/or after the competition ends.

Competition Round Template Example

Competition Name: The 2020 Mock Screenplay Contest
Competition Year: 2020

Round	1 of 5
Round Terminology	Preliminary Round
Judge Credentials	Professional Script Readers
What is Judged	All entries in their entirety
Number of Judges	One
Ranking Quantifier	Numerical Scores
Cumulative Rank	N.A.
Advancement Threshold	Scripts that score 60 or higher

Total Entries	6200
Judged this Round	6200 (100% of entries)
Number that Advance	1315
Percent that Advance	21% of all entries

Genre Entered	Drama
Total Genre Entries	1873
Judged this Round	1873 (100% of drama entries)
Number that Advance	379
Percent that Advance	20% of all drama entries

Genre Entered	Sci-Fi
Total Genre Entries	658
Judged this Round	658 (100% of sci-fi entries)
Number that Advance	127
Percent that Advance	19% of all sci-fi entries

Script Entered	The Next Best Screenplay, version 18.9
My Results, Drama	Advanced
My Results, Sci-Fi	Advanced

Competition Name:	The 2020 Mock Screenplay Contest
Competition Year:	2020

Round	2 of 5
Round Terminology	Preliminary Round
Judge Credentials	Professional Script Readers
What is Judged	Scripts that received a score of 60 or higher from the first round
Number of Judges	Two
Ranking Quantifier	Numerical Scores
Cumulative Rank	Yes
Advancement Threshold	Scripts that score 85+ from at least one Preliminary Round judge, or a total score of 160+ from two Preliminary Round judges

Total Entries	6200
Judged this Round	1315 (21% of entries)
Number that Advance	944
Percent that Advance	15% of all entries

Genre Entered	Drama
Total Genre Entries	1873
Judged this Round	379 (20% of drama entries)
Number that Advance	251
Percent that Advance	13% of all drama entries

Genre Entered	Sci-Fi
Total Genre Entries	658
Judged this Round	127 (19% of sci-fi entries)
Number that Advance	96
Percent that Advance	15% of all sci-fi entries

Script Entered	The Next Best Screenplay, version 18.9
My Results, Drama	Advanced
My Results, Sci-Fi	Advanced

Competition Name:	The 2020 Mock Screenplay Contest
Competition Year:	2020

Round	3 of 5
Round Terminology	Quarterfinal Round
Judge Credentials	Film Agents and Managers
What is Judged	Scripts that scored 85+ from at least one Preliminary Round judge, or a total score of 160+ from two Preliminary Round judges
Number of Judges	Two
Ranking Quantifier	Numerical Scores
Cumulative Rank	Yes
Advancement Threshold	Each script's lowest score is eliminated and the remaining 4 scores are combined. The top scoring 5% per genre advance

Total Entries	6200
Judged this Round	944 (15% of entries)
Number that Advance	310
Percent that Advance	5% of all entries

Genre Entered	Drama
Total Genre Entries	1873
Judged this Round	251 (13% of drama entries)
Number that Advance	94
Percent that Advance	5% of all drama entries

Genre Entered	Sci-Fi
Total Genre Entries	658
Judged this Round	96 (15% of sci-fi entries)
Number that Advance	33
Percent that Advance	5% of all sci-fi entries

Script Entered	The Next Best Screenplay, version 18.9
My Results, Drama	*Final Round Reached*
My Results, Sci-Fi	Advanced

Competition Name:	The 2020 Mock Screenplay Contest
Competition Year:	2020

Round	4 of 5
Round Terminology	Semifinal Round
Judge Credentials	Professional Screenwriters
What is Judged	The top scoring 5% of entries per genre
Number of Judges	Three
Ranking Quantifier	Numerical Scores
Cumulative Rank	Yes
Advancement Threshold	Each script's lowest score is eliminated and the remaining 7 scores are combined. The top scoring 5 scripts advance per genre

Total Entries	6200
Judged this Round	310 (5% of entries)
Number that Advance	50 (5 per genre)
Percent that Advance	0.0081% of all entries

Genre Entered	Drama
Total Genre Entries	1873
Judged this Round	94 (5% of drama entries)
Number that Advance	5
Percent that Advance	0.0027% of all drama entries

Genre Entered	Sci-Fi
Total Genre Entries	658
Judged this Round	33 (5% of sci-fi entries)
Number that Advance	5
Percent that Advance	0.0076% of all sci-fi entries

Script Entered	The Next Best Screenplay, version 18.9
My Results, Drama	N/A
My Results, Sci-Fi	*Final Round Reached*

Competition Name:	The 2020 Mock Screenplay Contest
Competition Year:	2020

Round	5 of 5
Round Terminology	Final Round
Judge Credentials	Top Film Producers
What is Judged	The top scoring 5 scripts per genre
Number of Judges	Five
Ranking Quantifier	Decisions
Cumulative Rank	No
Advancement Threshold	Judges read the finalist scripts then meet for discussion. Taking previous judges' ranks and comments into consideration, the Final Round judges select genre winners & 1 overall winner from those genre winners

Total Entries	6200
Judged this Round	50 (0.0081% of entries)
Number that Advance	1 Overall Winner
Percent that Advance	0.0002% of all entries

Genre Entered	Drama
Total Genre Entries	1873
Judged this Round	5 (0.0027% of drama entries)
Number that Advance	1 Winner
Percent that Advance	0.0005% of all drama entries

Genre Entered	Sci-Fi
Total Genre Entries	658
Judged this Round	5 (0.0076% of sci-fi entries)
Number that Advance	1
Percent that Advance	.0015% of all sci-fi entries

Script Entered	The Next Best Screenplay, version 18.9
My Results, Drama	N/A
My Results, Sci-Fi	N/A

25

The Submission Template

When I first started entering competitions, I didn't know what kind of information I should record. As a result, I don't have the information today that I wish I did about my initial entries. I now use the Submission Template for all my submissions and have found it incredibly helpful. And I honestly believe it will be beneficial for you, too.

While the previous two templates were designed to help *research* competitions, the Submission Template is meant to be used *during the submission process* and to maintain records of entries and your results.

I suggest completing the Submission Template *per calendar year* and/or *per year per script*.

You *could* complete this template per competition, but I like to have all the yearly data in one place. It makes it easier to see, at a glance, which competitions I've entered, those I still need to enter, and my results. Moreover, if I ever want to review my results in the future, either to see how my scripts ranked and/or so I can reference a placement in a pitch or query letter, then this template makes that process easier.

What follows is a Submission Template for 2018 entries of two feature scripts. I have fabricated the competitions and scripts in order to demonstrate how different information might be recorded on the Submission Template.

I've spread the template across four pages, but if you use a spreadsheet program, I suggest putting all fields on one sheet.

The Submission Template Example

Part A

Date Entered	Date Paid	Confirmations Received	Results Received	Critique Requested	Critique Received	Script Title	Script Version	Resubmission	Updated Version	Date Submitted	Replacement Tier
2/8/18	2/8/18	√	√	√	√	The Next Great Screenplay	18.9	NO			
3/12/18	3/12/18	√	√	NO	N/A	Amazing Screenplay	17.7	NO			
1/10/18	1/10/18	√	√	√	√	The Next Great Screenplay	18.9	NO	20.2	9/21/18	Semifinal Round
1/10/18	1/10/18	√	√	√	√	The Next Great Screenplay	18.9	NO			
1/10/18	1/10/18	√	√	√	√	The Next Great Screenplay	18.9	NO			
4/25/18	4/25/18	√	√	√	√	The Next Great Screenplay	20.2	YES			
1/10/18	1/10/18	√	√	N/A	N/A	The Next Great Screenplay	18.9	NO			
1/10/18	1/10/18	√	√	N/A	N/A	Amazing Screenplay	17.7	NO			

Part B		Part C			
Competition	**Year**	**Title Page**	**Additional Materials**	**Genre-Specific Judging**	**Genre / Category**
Example Fellowship, The 2018	2018	Title Only	Logline	NO	Drama, Sci-fi
Example Fellowship, The 2018	2018	Title Only	Logline	NO	Comedy, Family-friendly
Example Screenplay Competition, Fifteenth Annual	2018	Title Only	Logline	YES	Drama
Example Screenplay Competition, Fifteenth Annual	2018	Title Only	Logline	YES	Sci-fi
Made-up Contest 2018, The	2018	Title, Name & Contact	None	NO	N/A
Made-up Contest 2018, The	2018	Title, Name & Contact	None	NO	N/A
Pretend Screenplay Competition, The 2018	2018	Not specified. Incl. title & contact	Logline & short writer bio	YES	Sci-Fi
Pretend Screenplay Competition, The 2018	2018	Not specified. Incl. title & contact	Logline & short writer bio	YES	Family-friendly

Part D								Part E		
Entry Fee	Critique Fee	Discount Type	Discount Amount	Additional Purchases	Additional Fees	Paid Via	Total Paid	First Announcement	Results	Competition Scores
$45.00	$40.00					Visa	$85.00	8/1/18	Did Not Advance (bottom 60%)	Unspecified (less than 60)
$45.00	N/A					Visa	$45.00	8/1/18	Second Round (top 40%-16%)	First round judges = 79, 83 Second round judge = 80
$40.00	$79.00					Visa	$119.00	Mid Sept 2018	Semifinalist (top 5%)	N/A
$20.00	$79.00					Visa	$99.00	Mid Sept 2018	Did Not Advance (bottom 90%)	N/A
$60.00	Incl.			Book on screenwriting	$7.00	Visa	$67.00	5/3/18	Did Not Advance (percentage unknown)	N/A
$30.00	Incl.					Visa	$30.00	5/3/18	Quarterfinalist (percentage unknown)	N/A
$50.00	N/A	Entered Previously	-$10.00			Visa	$40.00	7/15/18	Second Round (top 11%-25%)	First round judge = 69 Second round judge = 71
$50.00	N/A	Multiple Entry Disc	-$5.00	2 more First Round Judges	$30.00	Visa	$75.00	7/15/18	Quarterfinalist (top 10%-6%)	First round judges = 92, 76, 84 Second round judge = 83 Third round judge = 79

Part F					Part G
Critique Release	**Critique by Judge**	**Critic Credentials**	**Critique Scores**	**Critique Summary**	**Misc. Information**
7/4/2018 by 12:00am	YES	Professional Script Readers	Unspecified (less than 60)	2 received. Contrary comments re: characters' believability Both agree pacing needs work. Both agree in script's potential.	
N/A	N/A	N/A	N/A	N/A	Two judges in round one, one judge in round two.
After elimination	NO	Years of judging, prof. writing or teaching	Concept 7, Format 10, Structure 8, Plot 7, Pacing 6, Characters 7, Dialogue 7, Theme 5, Style 7, Commercial Potential 6. Pass=script, Recommend=writer	Liked protagonist but wanted a more layered antagonist. Thought the theme should be explored more.	Sent updated version for semifinal round judging. Previous ranks remained in effect.
After elimination	NO	Years of judging, prof. writing or teaching	Concept 9, Format 10, Structure 7, Plot 7, Pacing 8, Characters 7, Dialogue 9, Theme 6, Style 8, Commercial Potential 6. Pass	Loved the concept. Thought the theme should unfold through more action and less exposition.	Entry fee only $20 since was a second genre.
4/1/18	YES, 1st round	Unknown	N/A	Liked concept. Didn't connect to characters.	
5/25/18	YES, 1st round	Unknown	N/A	Liked concept. Liked character arcs. Wanted less exposition.	For resubmission I requested the same first-round judge who had judged the script initially.
N/A	N/A	N/A	N/A	N/A	
N/A	N/A	N/A	N/A	N/A	Purchased judging from three first round judges. Only one first round judge advanced script to second round.

The Submission Template Explained

The Submission Template is divided into seven parts for explanatory purposes.

You will complete each *row of fields* per competition *per script entered*. If you enter more than one script (or more than one version of a script) into a single competition, then treat each of those as a separate row on the template.

If the competition uses genre or category-specific judging and you enter a script into *more* than one genre/category, record *each genre/category as a separate entry*, so you can track the results of your script *per* genre/category (since your script may advance further in one genre/category than another).

If a field doesn't apply to your entry, enter "N/A" (not applicable) or "NO." This is because, in the future, it's helpful to see that the information didn't apply (otherwise, you might think you simply forgot to record the information).

Finally, I sort this template alphabetically by competition name. Since the majority of competitions include the competition *year* in their name (e.g. "The 2020 Mock Screenplay Contest"), I place the year at the end of the competition's name (e.g. "Mock Screenwriting Competition, The 2020").

Part A

Columns in Part A serve as a "quick reference" so you can quickly see the per-competition status of your entries, results, and critiques.

Date Entered. Record the date that you entered the competition. This would be the date you submitted your script, entry form, and other requested materials (not necessarily the date you submitted payment).

Date Paid. Record the date you *paid* for your submission. Typically this will be the same date that you entered your script in the competition, but if you're mailing any part of your submission, or phoning in your payment, the dates might be slightly different.

Confirmations Received. An entry isn't final until the competition has processed *all* submission materials (e.g. entry and payment). Once you receive confirmations for both your script entry and payment, place a check mark in this field.

Results Received. Once you receive your script's final competition results (once your script has been eliminated from, or wins, the competition) place a check mark in this field.

Critique Requested. If you requested/purchased a critique in conjunction with your competition entry, place a check mark or "YES" in this field.

If you did not request/purchase a critique, enter "NO."

If the competition does not offer critiques in conjunction with competition entries, enter "N/A."

If you can request/purchase competition-related critiques *after* you enter the competition, use this field to record that applicable date range.

Critique Received. Add a check mark to this field when you receive your critique/s. If the competition does not offer critiques (or if you did not request/purchase the critiques offered), enter "N/A."

Script Title. Record the title of the script you entered.

Script Version. Record the version of the script entered. This is helpful because you might enter more than one version of your script (either in that same year or in a future year) and by recording the version, you can refer back to see how the different versions ranked.

Resubmission. If you send a resubmission that will be judged separately from your original entry, record that resubmission *as a separate entry on the Submission Template* and enter "YES" here.

Updated Version. If you send an updated version of your script to the competition that *replaces* the original entry (for some or all of the competition) use this field to record the version number of the updated script.

Date Submitted. Record the date you submitted the updated version.

Replacement Tier. Record the competition tier (or round) in which your updated script replaced your original script (e.g. third round, quarterfinal round, final round).

Part B

The two columns in Part B help keep accurate records relative to each script and competition entered.

Competition. Record the *official* name of the competition.

Year. Record the *competition year* (this may not be the year you *entered* the competition).

Part C

The information needed to complete these four columns can usually be found in the competition's eligibility and submission requirements, rules, guidelines, etc.

Title Page. Enter the competition's title page requirements. If the competition is not specific or if they accept different options, then record the option you used.

Additional Materials. Indicate if you submitted any additional materials as part of your entry (e.g. writer biography, a letter explaining why you want to be a screenwriter, a logline or summary, list of recurring characters).

While not included on the example template, you could indicate whether any of the additional materials will be used for judging and/or promotional purposes.

Genre-Specific Judging. Record whether the competition uses genre-specific (or format/category-specific) judging.

Genre/Category. Record the genre/category under which you entered your script.

Even if the competition doesn't use genre or category-specific judging, if my script's genre/category is requested on the entry form, then I still record the genres/categories I indicated because judges are sometimes assigned scripts by genre/category-preference. Recording the genres/categories I enter my script under might help me determine in which genres/categories my script typically ranks the best.

If you're entering a teleplay, I might split this one field into two: one for category (which would be for pilots or specs) and the other for genre (which could be comedy and drama, or 30-minute and 60-minute). But, again, the genre lines for teleplays are becoming increasingly blurred, so find a record-keeping system that makes sense to you and then keep clear and consistent notes.

Part D

Payment information is recorded in Part D. Odds are you won't reference this information much in the future, but this part of the template is helpful during the submission process and for bookkeeping purposes.

Entry Fee. Record the cost to enter your script in the competition (or the cost of the resubmission).

Critique Fee. If you purchase a critique, enter that cost here. If critiques are included with the entry fee, enter "Incl." If you will not receive a critique in correlation with your entry, enter "N/A."

Discount Type. If you apply a discount (coupon, special rate, etc.), explain how you obtained that discount, For example, "Entered competition prior year," or "Black Friday coupon."

Discount Amount. Record the dollar amount of the savings from the Discount Type field.

Additional Purchases. Explain any additional purchases you made in conjunction with your entry (e.g. books offered by the competition organization or festival passes).

Additional Fees. Record the total dollar amount of the additional purchases noted in the Additional Purchases field.

Paid Via. Record the method you used to pay for your submission (e.g. credit card, check, PayPal).

Total Paid. The total dollar amount paid for all entry-related fees. This should be the combined total of the entry fee, critique fee, and additional purchases, less any discounts.

Part E

Part E is devoted to your *competition results*.

First Announcement. Record the date you expect the first advancement announcement. You can add to this field (or create a separate column) to record *how* those announcements will be made (e.g. online, email, letter, phone call).

Later, if you advance in a competition, you can update this field (or add a new column) to reflect the date of the *next* advancement announcement.

Results. Complete this field once you know your script's final rank.

If your script doesn't reach an advancement tier, but you know how many rounds it advanced through, record that here. For example, I've had scripts that advanced past the first round reader at PAGE but did not make the quarterfinals. In this case I would enter, "Advanced to the second round."

If your script does not advance through any rounds of competition, enter "Did not advance."

If your script doesn't win the competition and the competition does not provide any information pertaining to how many rounds and/or advancement tiers your script advanced through, enter "Not specified" and/or "Did not place."

Finally, if the competition provides the numbers and/or percentages of how many scripts made up your placement level, record that information in this field. For example, "quarterfinalist—top 25%" or "quarterfinalist—between the top 10% and 25% of entries in this genre."

Competition Scores. If you receive your script's score/s record them here so you can easily determine in which competitions (and hopefully in which genres) your script scored best.

I suggest including any and all scores (total and/or per criteria) so you can easily reference which scripts (and/or versions) excelled in which judging criteria. This information should help you improve your script and determine a trend in your writing as a whole (e.g. maybe you always score high on characters or dialogue).

Part F

The columns in Part F are devoted to the *results of your written critique*. If you did not request or purchase a critique in conjunction with your entry, or if the competition did not offer written critiques, then enter "N/A" for the following fields.

Critique Release. This is the date you expect to receive your critique. For example, May 1st, 2020, or after elimination/win. If the expected receipt date is "4 weeks after submission" then when you know your entry date you can calculate the actual *calendar date* you should receive your critique and record that here.

Critique by Judge. Indicate whether the critique/s will be written by your script's competition judge/s. If the competition doesn't specify, simply enter "Unknown."

Critic Credentials. Record the credentials of your critic/s in this field.

Critique Scores. Enter your critique scores here. If your critique was not written by your script's judge in the competition, these scores likely won't match your script's competition scores.

If you receive a total score and criteria-specific scores with your critique, I suggest recording both.

Critique Summary. Enter a quick summary of your critique (e.g. whether the critique was overall positive, what the main suggestions for improvement were, if your script was assigned a *Pass*, *Consider*, or *Recommend*, if the critic made any comments about your writing skills as a whole).

Part G

Misc. Information. Use this field for any additional notes you may want to add. This could be anything unique about the competition, your entry, or your critique. Maybe you want to record that you paid for more than one first round judge. Maybe you want to record the prizes you won for placing in the competition. Maybe you want to remind yourself to watch for a coupon emailed a few months after the final announcement. Whatever you want to remember or reference in the future can be recorded here.

Glossary

Advance/Advancement. A script surviving elimination and moving on to the next round of competition.

Advancement Announcement. An advancement announcement occurs when a competition publicly announces which scripts have reached an advancement tier.

Advancement Threshold. The rank a script must achieve in order to advance in the competition.

Advancement Tier. A level of advancement in which the competition publicly announces the scripts that reached a certain level of the competition. Each advancement tier could consist of one or many competition rounds. Typically advancement tiers are: quarterfinals, semifinals, finals, and winners.

Alumni. Writers who have won or placed in a competition.

Application Process. *See* Submission Process.

Award Level. A placement within a competition that's accompanied by one or more prizes.

Category. A classification used for judging and award purposes that is not a typical format or genre (e.g. "best female protagonist" or "best script by a student"). Often competitions will use the term *category*, *genre*, and *format* interchangeably.

Category-Specific Judging. Scripts judged only against other scripts in the same category rather than judging all categories of scripts together.

Competition Round. A portion of the competition in which a batch of scripts are read, evaluated and ranked. Those rankings (or those rankings in addition to the script's rankings in previous rounds) determine which scripts advance in the competition. Once those advancements (and corresponding eliminations) are made, the next "round" begins. A competition may have several rounds per advancement tier.

Competition Year. The way in which a competition distinguishes between past and current competition periods (usually either the year the competition opens for entries or the year they announce the winner/s). Some competitions don't reference calendar years, but instead reference the number of times the competition has been held (e.g. twentieth annual competition).

Criteria. The aspects of a script that each judge/critic should use to evaluate a script's strengths and weaknesses for ranking/critiquing purposes (as set forth by the competition). Typically these criteria are accompanied by explanations and guidance from the competition organizers as to what would cause a script to receive a high or low rank for each criterion.

Critic. The individual who writes your critique. This may or may not be your script's judge in the competition. Sometimes competitions refer to critics as *judges* or *readers*.

Critique Criteria. The aspects of a script that each critic should use to evaluate a script's strengths and weaknesses for critiquing purposes (as set forth by the competition). Typically these criteria are accompanied by explanations and guidance from the competition organizers as to what would cause a script to receive a positive or negative evaluation for each criterion.

Critique Service. Written critiques offered (typically for a fee) by the competition (or the competition's organization). These may or may not be related to the competition itself.

Entrant. A writer or contributor who submitted material to the competition for judging. Sometimes referred to as *applicant*.

Entry/Entries. The intellectual material submitted to a competition to be judged. Usually a full and complete script. Please note that sometimes "entry" refers to all materials required for submission to a competition—*see* Submission and Submission Process for more.

Entry Form. The page (or pages) entrants are required to complete and submit to a competition in order to enter. The information required typically pertains to the writer, the entered script, information regarding the entrant's previous entries (if applicable), and the entrant's agreement to the competition's fine print.

Entry Process. *See* Submission Process.

Fine Print. The rules, requirements, terms and conditions, privacy policies, agreements, guidelines, etc., that an entrant must agree to when entering a competition.

Format. The medium for which a script was written: e.g. feature film, short film, television. Format can also refer to sub-formats, like spec scripts vs. shooting scripts, or teleplay pilots vs. teleplay specs.

Format-Specific Judging. Scripts judged only against other scripts in the same format rather than judging all formats of scripts together.

Genre. Genre refers to the typical styles and subject matters associated with a kind of story (for example, science fiction, thriller, horror, drama, comedy, etc.). Some competitions refer to genre as *category*.

Genre-Specific Judging. Scripts judged only against other scripts in the same genre rather than judging all genres of scripts together.

Judge. Any individual who reads and ranks your script for a competition and has a say in whether your script advances. Sometimes competitions refer to judges as *readers*. Sometimes competitions refer to critics as *judges*.

Judging Criteria. The aspects of a script that each judge should use to evaluate a script's strengths and weaknesses for ranking purposes. Typically these criteria are accompanied by explanations and guidance from the competition organizers as to what would cause a script to receive a high or low rank for each criterion.

Logline. A logline is a short (about a paragraph) summary of your script's story and/or concept.

Place/Placement. A level of advancement in the competition correlating to an advancement tier, e.g. a quarterfinalist, semifinalist, finalist.

Quantifier/s. The measurable ranking a judge uses to translate his/her assessment of a script's qualities. Usually quantifiers are one or a combination of the following: scores, recommendations for advancement or elimination, comments about the script, discussion among judges.

Rank. The level a judge assigns a script based on the script's strengths and weaknesses often relative to the competition's judging criteria.

Reader. *See* Judge.

Resubmission. A resubmission occurs when you submit a new version of a script that you've already entered in the competition that will, typically, be judged as a new entry, separate from your original entry.

Round. *See* Competition Round.

Submission. All required materials (scripts, payments, entry forms, etc.) that must be submitted to a competition in order to participate in the competition. Sometimes referred to as *entry* or *application*.

Submission Period. The time frame during which a competition accepts entries.

Submission Process. The act of sending all required materials and payment to a competition. Sometimes referred to as *entry process* and/or *application process*.

Threshold. *See* Advancement Threshold.

Tone. The style, feel (happy, sad, hopeful, tragic, etc.), and amount of light or dark within a script. For example, you could have a script that is in the "comedy" genre, but it could be a "dark" comedy or a "light" comedy.

Written Critique. A written evaluation of your script.

Index

H-I

J

K-L

M

N

O